CONTENTS

A SLICE OF AMERICA'S BOUNTY

It wasn't until the bicentennial in 1976 that our nation really rediscovered "American food." Fueled by a long, nostalgic look at our past and its traditions, we began to recognize that American cuisine consisted of more than just fast-food burgers, hot dogs, and meat loaf, and that American cooking was thriving in unique and infinite variety. In the good old days, before all the hoopla started, we called our recipes by their proper names—Aunt Martha's Pot Roast, Grandma's Chicken Casserole, Uncle Bert's Secret Barbecue Sauce. American cooking was a quiet sort of tradition back then—recipes exchanged over church suppers and quilting bees, passed along from mother to daughter to neighbor to friend.

But the world began to move a little faster, and the tradition has attracted quite a bit more noisy attention than Grandma ever dreamed possible. Lately the regionalists have jumped on the bandwagon, touting everything from Tex-Mex chili to Creole gumbo to Maryland crabs as being representative of what "real" American food is all about.

Yet in the midst of it all, somebody forgot to mention pie.

Pies—piled high with fresh fruit or rich with cream—have been cooling on American windowsills since the colonial days. Perhaps no single product of this country's cooking is more indigenous or more inspiring. After all, it was Mom's Apple Pie that sent soldiers into battle. Though admittedly biased, it's hard for me to imagine a mere chicken leg or a bowl of chili inspiring the same sort of patriotic fervor. With all due respect, I maintain that pies are what American food is really about. Regional chauvinism aside, pie baking has thrived in every area of the country since its beginnings. Southern pecans, berries from Eastern forests, cream from Midwestern dairies, bountiful fruit harvests from backyard orchards and gardens, nearly everything America has to offer in the way of native ingredients has found its way into a pie crust at one time or another. Pie-baking competitions and pie-eating contests have been part of the American tradition from Bangor to Baton Rouge. Slices of pie are proudly and

WHO'S WHO

Great pies are a tradition in my family. Some of the recipes here date from my great-grandmother, Dovie. Over the years, she passed her baking skills on to her daughters, Jessie Lou and Baby, my grandmother and great-aunt. The third generation is well represented by my mother, Virginia, who in turn brought Grandma Renata's German and Russian influence to bear on the family's repertoire of recipes. Then Aunt Dear joined the clan with some formidable talent of her own. Most of what I know about pie baking I learned in their kitchens, peering over their shoulders, helping out, and doing some experimenting of my own. The recipes here represent their best.

temptingly displayed everywhere, from the most elegant restaurants to the humblest roadside diner. Country kitchen or city bakery, the pie is always in demand.

The pie recipes here are truly representative of that broad and varied tradition. They are pies that have gone to bake sales and church suppers, graced holiday tables, and been eaten and enjoyed by nearly four generations of one American family, their neighbors, and their friends. Like most American families these days, we are scattered throughout the country. Our recipes come from all over. But whether they are Northern, Southern, or Midwestern in origin, they remain distinctly American in flavor and character. These pies are products of that quieter cooking tradition, recipes I've called by their proper names: Aunt Dear's Pecan Creme Pie, Mom's Apple, Jessie Lou's Favorite—the list goes on. In so doing, I hope that my tradition will become part of yours.

So whether you live in Iowa or Idaho, whether your idea of good eating is clam chowder or catfish, burgers or beef stew, don't forget to finish your meals with a true all-American flourish—a mouthwatering slice of American Pie.

Teresa Kennedy

STARTING OFF

PREPARING FOR GREAT PIES

PREPARING FOR GREAT PIES

I want to let you in on the best-kept secret of pie baking: it's easy! After all, they don't use the expression "easy as pie" for nothing. You don't need to be a genius, a food expert, or even an experienced baker to get great results your first time out. What you do need are fresh, wholesome ingredients, a minimum of kitchen equipment, and, of course, good recipes. The information in this chapter will give you a head start; the hints, pointers, and general discussion are designed to give you the benefits of years of baking experience in a few short pages. They will help steer you to the right utensils, the right ingredients, and the right techniques. Read them over before beginning your recipe, refer to them as you need them, and whether you're novice or expert, I can all but guarantee you the pie of your dreams!

BAKING UTENSILS

Utensils for pie baking range from the very minimal to some fairly elaborate kitchen gadgetry. My own preferences fall somewhere in the middle. The important thing is to have utensils and equipment that you feel comfortable using and can depend on.

Pastry Blenders: A pastry blender is a hand-held tool that is specially designed for cutting shortening into flour. It consists of five or six wires attached at both ends to a handle, forming a wide loop. I don't favor the use of a blender for a couple of reasons: first of all, it takes too long to blend pastry using it—giving the shortening time to get too warm for a good crust; and second, a good crust is best achieved by learning how the pastry should feel—which you can't do unless you use your fingers.

Rolling Pins: Choose the type of rolling pin that is easiest for you to handle. I tend to prefer the old style that consists of a cylinder of wood, usually about 3 inches in diameter, with a small handle on each end. Other types of rolling pins include a smaller, lighter version that is somewhat longer, about 1½ inches in diameter and tapered at the ends. This type has a rougher finish and is meant to be used with a cover or a pastry cloth. With traditional pins, a smooth, satiny finish is essential, with no scars or dents. I recommend checking your local antique stores or auctions for a rolling pin that is seasoned and in good condition. Just make sure it isn't warped and that it rolls smoothly. Other types of rolling pins include ones made of marble, which are impressive but awfully heavy, and pins with a built-in ruler so you can measure the dough as you roll it out.

Rolling Pin Covers: A rolling pin cover consists of a sleeve, usually cheesecloth, that fits over the cylinder of the rolling pin.

It is nice to have, since it prevents dough from sticking or getting tough from having too much flour worked into it.

Pastry Boards: Pastry boards come in a variety of materials—wood, marble, and hard plastic being the most common. The average board looks just like a chopping board except that it is larger. It's nice to have a pastry board if you have the space, but it's not really necessary. (Never roll out crusts on a chopping board you have used for strong-flavored foods such as onions, garlic, or fish.)

Pastry Cloths: Pastry cloths come in muslin, cheesecloth, and a disposable paper version. They prevent the dough from sticking to your work surface. And since the cloth holds a certain amount of flour, you are less tempted to overflour the work surface and rolling pin, which would result in a tough crust. To use, lay the pastry cloth on your work surface and flour it very lightly. Place the dough in the center of the cloth and proceed as per the rolling hints on page 20.

Pie Pans: I think it has been statistically proven someplace that the average American household boasts one slightly dented pie pan of indeterminate size that is hauled out once a year on Thanksgiving. If this is true at your house, sorry, but things will have to change if you're going to get serious about pie baking, because the first thing you'll need are good pie pans. Here are some pointers for making the all-important investment.

Glass Pans. In general, glass, Pyrex, or Corning-type ceramic pans are my first choice for baking pies. They are particularly good for baking filled crusts. Since they tend to distribute heat faster than do metal pans, they prevent the soggy bottom crusts often caused by fruit, nut, and custard-type fillings. However, it may be necessary to reduce your oven temperature by as much as 25°F to prevent too-rapid baking.

Aluminum Pans. Heavy aluminum pans are my second choice for pie baking. The trick is to turn a new aluminum pan into an old aluminum pan. You know the kind: knife marks on the bottom and slightly blackened with age. After all, most of the recipes in this cookbook were first baked in the old standby aluminum pie pans my grandmothers, mother, and aunts picked up at the five-and-dime. However, if you find yourself stuck with one that is shiny-new, here's how to season it: Wash the pan really well in hot soapy water and dry it thoroughly. Preheat the oven to 425° F, and rub the bottom and sides of the pan with cooking oil. Bake the empty pan for 20 minutes. The surface should darken somewhat, which is what we're after. A darkened pan distributes heat more evenly.

Finished Pans. Pie pans that have been coated with Teflon II or another finish such as Baker's Secret are really not very useful. Pies are generally served directly from the pan in which they are baked, and it is nearly impossible to slice a pie in one of these pans without harming the special finish.

They do make for easy cleanup, but if you've rolled out the crust properly, there shouldn't be much of a problem with leakage or baked-on filling in the first place.

Foil Pans. I must confess that when testing and perfecting some of the recipes here, I gave in and used a number of throwaway foil pie pans. Even a dedicated cook like myself can wash only so many pans in one lifetime! I recommend them for pre-baked crusts, crumb crusts, and for those occasions when your pies have some traveling to do and you don't want to haul your good pie pans back and forth. Don't use foil pans for any pie that goes into the oven with a liquid filling, like custard or baked cream. These are too heavy for the pan, making it impossible to move the pie from counter to oven without spilling some.

Baking Beans: These are generally found in department and specialty stores. They are small round clay, ceramic, or aluminum pieces, designed to weight down unfilled pie pastry as it bakes, eliminating the need to prick the crust. The clay distributes the heat quickly and evenly over the crust; the beans also prevent warping, bubbling, and to a lesser extent, shrinkage during baking. Although some home bakers like to use dried beans such as navy or kidney beans to weight down crusts, I don't recommend it. Since you can't use these beans for eating afterwards, you wind up just wasting them.

Electric Mixers: I generally specify the use of a hand-held electric mixer in my recipes because they are somewhat easier to maneuver than the stationary variety. If you are using a stationary mixer, reduce the mixing speeds given here. High speed on a hand-held mixer, for example, would be medium or medium-low on a stationary one.

Double Boilers: To make cooked pie fillings (Lemon Meringue, Black Bottom, Natural Key Lime, etc.), it is a good idea to invest in a double boiler. A double boiler consists of two pots, one of which is designed to fit on top of the other. The bottom pot is filled with 2 to 2½ inches of water and as it simmers, it steam-cooks whatever is in the top section. This gentle cooking prevents scorching and lumping. There are any number of brands of cookware that include double boilers, but I recommend a copper-bottom pot with a ceramic or porcelain inner section, because copper heats faster and the ceramic or porcelain maintains an even cooking temperature.

If you don't have a double boiler, you can make do with any small pot that fits inside a larger one, so long as it sits above the water level. It may be necessary to adjust the cooking time in this case. If you're using a makeshift double boiler, a word of warning: Wear a heavy potholder glove that covers your hand and forearm as you stir your pie fillings—steam or splashing can burn badly.

Oven Thermometers: Any experienced cook knows that the thermostat on the oven doesn't necessarily have anything to do with the temperature inside the oven. Oven temperature can be affected by any number of factors, including the age of the stove and whether or not the burners are in use. Even your oven cleaning habits can throw the temperature off, so unless you are an experienced baker and can predict the necessary adjustments, buy a good oven thermometer.

PIE INGREDIENTS

If there's one instance where the maxim "You get what you pay for" applies, it's in good cooking. Never, never, skimp on quality for the sake of price when it comes to fresh, wholesome ingredients for your pies. Buy the best you can find and let your tastebuds tell the story.

Flour: Unless otherwise specified, use white all-purpose sifted flour in these recipes. In pastry-making particularly, never substitute self-rising or cake flour for all-purpose flour. Whenever possible, I recommend the use of unbleached white flour rather than the more refined bleached variety because of its greater nutritional value and flavor.

Butter: I favor the use of lightly salted butter in most recipes, and particularly for pastry-making. Pie crust made without salt just doesn't taste like anything. If you prefer, substitute unsalted butter in filling recipes; but even if you're watching your salt intake, be sure to add a small amount of salt substitute or a pinch of salt if you're using unsalted butter in a crust recipe.

Vegetable Shortening: Some national food-store chains do have good-quality house brands of vegetable shortening, but in general bargain brands in shortening aren't a good idea. Often bargain-brand or generic shortenings are made from reprocessed oils, with a real sacrifice in quality and flavor. Read the label. Make sure the shortening you buy is pure, all-vegetable, and recommended for baking.

Contrary to popular belief, shortening doesn't last forever on the shelf. If yours has been around for more than a couple of months, taste it before using it. There should be no oily flavor and no aftertaste.

Lard: My mother insists that she can remember the days when rendered lard was bought by the bucket from the local butcher at the astonishing price of three cents a pail. Those days are gone, but you can still buy lard in 1-pound blocks at the local supermarket. Always use rendered lard, and always check package dates to ensure a fresh product. Though lard does not require refrigeration, it's a good idea to keep it cool, and refrigeration will extend its keeping qualities somewhat.

Sugar: When more than one kind of sugar is used in a recipe, I have specified the types: brown, confectioners' (powdered), granulated. If the type isn't specified, use granulated.

If you run out of brown sugar, add ¼ cup molasses to ¾ cup granulated sugar to make 1 cup of firmly packed brown sugar.

Fruit: Use fresh, ripe fruit whenever possible. Of course, you needn't give up your favorite peach pie just because it's December; just substitute frozen fruit instead. Try to get unsweetened frozen fruit if you can, but if not, simply cut the amount of sugar in your favorite filling recipe accordingly. Fresh or frozen, always taste your fruit before adding sugar. While the amounts of sugar called for in these recipes are a good guideline, they can't serve you as well as your own tastebuds can. Increase or decrease the amount of sugar by as much as ¼ cup when using fresh fruit; decrease by as much as ½ cup when using sweetened frozen fruit.

Chocolate: Whether a recipe calls for unsweetened, semi-sweet, or sweet chocolate, the result will depend on the quality of chocolate you use. Never, never, *never* use artificially flavored chocolate products, and don't use bargain-brand chocolate chips. They don't melt properly and the flavor just doesn't compare to the real thing. If you are price conscious, buy bulk chocolate (generally priced by the pound and cheaper than brand-name products) and make your own chips in the food processor.

PIE FACT

Often you may find yourself a little shy on fruit for pie filling. No need to put off your baking: just be careful not to overpower the filling with too much crust. Top with a lattice crust rather than a full top crust. Also, don't be afraid to combine fruits—the results are almost always wonderful (see Great Fruit Pie Combinations, page 42)!

Eggs: I have used large or extra-large eggs in my recipes. If you use medium eggs, either add an extra egg or compensate with the addition of 4 tablespoons milk.

For beaten egg whites in meringues and fillings, always use large or extra-large eggs, and always use egg whites that have been brought to room temperature for fluffy, spectacular results.

Cream: Cream comes in three varieties: light, heavy or whipping, and half-and-half. In recipes that call for small amounts of light cream, half-and-half can be substituted in nearly all instances. For cream pies and recipes that call for more than 1 cup of light cream, there may be some variations in texture and setting qualities when half-and-half is used. Heavy cream is used for whipping, but be careful not to use heavy cream that has been ultrapasteurized. It isn't as flavorful as regular cream and doesn't whip well.

About Thickeners: In some form or other, thickeners are an important ingredient in almost every pie filling.

Cornstarch. Cornstarch tends to provide a nicer texture for a pie filling than does flour, but it can pose problems for less experienced cooks. This is my rule of thumb: In cream pies and cooked pie fillings, use cornstarch wherever possible. In fruit pies or custards that bake in the crust, use flour. Flour is easier to blend and doesn't require an extended baking time at a low temperature. Fruit pies baked with cornstarch can be undependable. Though the pie may look baked and the fruit seem tender, cornstarch that has not been baked long enough can ruin your work by adding an unpleasant flavor.

In the good old days, regulating the heat of a burner was often difficult, and most of the old recipes for cornstarch fillings recommend using a double boiler because it tends to slow down the cooking time. On our stoves, however, cornstarch fillings may be cooked in a regular saucepan on a *very low* setting, providing that the mixture is stirred constantly—and I mean constantly. It may look as if nothing's happening, but cornstarch is tricky that way. It thickens all at once, and you can wind up with a lumpy mess if you don't watch what you're doing.

If the phone rings while you're preparing your cornstarch filling and you do wind up with a few lumps, don't panic. Simply remove the saucepan from the heat and whisk out the lumps. Return it to the heat and finish the recipe. For more serious lumping problems, add 2 tablespoons of water to the mixture and beat with an electric mixer on high speed for 2 to 3 minutes, or until the mixture is smooth once again.

Flour. If you do choose flour over cornstarch as a thickening agent for cooked pie fillings, the method for cooking is the same: Make a paste of flour and liquid before adding it to the pie filling, and cook until thick, stirring constantly. Instant flours are great for both cooked fillings and baked fillings. They blend better and faster and therefore cut down on lumping and starchiness.

If you don't have instant flour on hand, blend all-purpose flour with club soda rather than water for absolutely lump-free paste. The carbonation disperses the flour for blending but doesn't affect the texture of the filling.

Egg Yolks. Many chilled pie fillings are thickened with cooked egg yolks or with a combination of egg yolks and unflavored gelatin. Always beat egg yolks thoroughly before cooking and always cook egg yolk fillings in the top of a double boiler. If you stir a small amount of the heated mixture into the egg yolks before adding the yolks to the hot mixture, this should prevent the yolks from curdling. Egg yolk fillings also must be stirred constantly to prevent curdling or lumping. A properly cooked egg yolk filling will be thick enough to coat a spoon and will mound just slightly when dropped from the spoon.

Gelatin. Gelatin fillings are made in

PIE FACT

In some areas of the country, light cream can be difficult to find. In many instances, half-and-half (half cream, half milk) can be substituted with no discernible difference, but in cream pies and those recipes that require more than 1 cup of cream there will be slight variations in texture.

two stages. First the gelatin must be softened in cold water before it is added to the rest of the filling mixture, and then the mixture is cooked in a double boiler. A gelatin filling should not be overcooked, however, or the result will be rubbery. In fillings that use both egg yolks and gelatin, the egg yolks are added and cooked first, the gelatin added last. Cook this mixture only until it is thick enough to coat a spoon and all gelatin granules are dissolved.

Most gelatin fillings are chilled until partially set, and then remaining ingredients such as beaten egg whites or whipped cream are folded into the chilled mixture; then the pie is refrigerated until the filling is completely set.

Tapioca. Tapioca is used as a thickener primarily for fruit pies and in cooked puddings. It can be substituted for flour in most fruit pie recipes by using about 1 tablespoon less tapioca than the amount of flour called for. Always use minute or instant tapioca rather than the larger pearl variety. Toss the fruit together with the sugar and tapioca and allow the mixture to stand for 15 minutes before placing it in an unbaked crust. Bake as usual.

THE PERFECT CRUSTS

PIE CRUST POINTERS
11 PERFECT CRUSTS

PIE CRUST POINTERS

"But I can't make pie crust!" is an oft-heard complaint. Nonsense—anyone can make pie crust. All you have to remember is one simple rule: Less is more. The main cause of crust failure lies in overdoing it—overmixing, overrolling, overflouring. Let these pointers serve as a troubleshooting guide and you'll never have to suffer a store-bought crust again!

BLENDING

Two of the most important things to remember when making pie crust are to use chilled ingredients and not to overblend. Shortening that is too warm combines with flour and water too easily and makes for a tough crust. The shortening (or butter or lard) used in pastry should never be completely incorporated into the flour. Small pockets of shortening should form in between the layers of flour paste, actually frying them as it bakes. This is what forms a flaky crust.

When using chilled vegetable shortening in making your pie crust, it is often difficult to measure it out smoothly without its becoming too soft. Here is an easy, unmessy way to measure shortening: Fill a measuring cup with 1 cup water, and add shortening until the water level rises to the amount of shortening called for plus 1 cup. For example, when you've added enough shortening to 1 cup of water to raise the level to 1⅔ cups, you have ⅔ cup shortening. Dump out the water and add the perfectly measured shortening to the flour. (Very little water clings to the shortening, so it is not necessary to pat it dry.)

I have found that the best way to blend a light crust is the old-fashioned way: with your fingers. After a little practice, you will be able to tell by the feel of it what is the correct texture for pie pastry and when a dough is blended enough. Cut the chilled shortening into the flour in small chunks, about 1-tablespoon size. Toss the shortening lightly in the flour to coat it, and gently roll the mixture between your fingers. Continue tossing and blending with your fingers, taking up more flour as you go, until the mixture has the texture of coarse fresh bread crumbs. Sprinkle the water over the entire surface of the crumb mixture and again work it with your fingers, only until the ingredients are just moistened. Gently form the dough into a ball. If the dough is crumbly, add 1 to 2 tablespoons more water, but remember—don't overblend.

Pie crust also can be made in a food processor fitted with a steel knife. Just keep the basic rules for pastry-making in mind and don't overprocess. Place all the ingredients, including the water, into the machine at once, before processing. Process only until the ingredients are lightly blended and the dough can be shaped, 15 to 20 seconds, depending on the speed of your machine. If yours has a pulse switch, use it to regulate the blending. Processor pastry does tend to require just a bit more moisture than hand-blended pastry. If necessary, you can increase the water in the recipe by as much as 1 tablespoon.

If you think you have overblended your pastry, you can remedy the situation by adding a teaspoon or two of cider vinegar to the dough. The vinegar will tenderize the flour somewhat during baking.

ROLLING

Chilling your pie dough before rolling it out isn't always necessary, but it can be a good idea if the day (or your kitchen!) is unusually warm. With butter-base crusts, though, chilling is almost always necessary as it helps to prevent these more fragile pastries from tearing during the rolling process.

The lightly floured surface called for in the majority of these recipes is just that. Spread only about ⅛ cup of flour over your work surface. Keep additional flour handy to lightly dust the rolling pin as you go. Dust the top of a pastry crust only if the dough is unusually moist. If you tend to be heavy-handed in flouring, invest in a pastry cloth and rolling pin cover.

Flatten the dough slightly with the heel

of your hand, then roll it out from the center in short, swift strokes. If your work surface is small, turn the dough in a circular pattern as you work to ensure even rolling.

If your pastry has a tendency to tear at the edges during rolling, it is for one of two reasons: you may be bearing down too heavily in the center of the dough, or your dough may be too dry. Wait until the dough is in the pie pan to mend breaks or tears. Moisten your fingertips with a little water or lightly beaten egg white and pinch the edges of the tear together.

Roll bottom crusts to a thickness of about ⅛ inch, and approximately 1½ inches larger than the diameter of your pie pan. Top crusts should be rolled to a thickness of $1/16$ inch and about 2 inches larger than the diameter of the pie pan. Dough for lattice crusts should be rolled to the same thickness as bottom crusts, to make the strips easy to handle and weave without tearing.

Some pastries that have sugar or butter added can be sticky to roll. Rather than risk incorporating too much flour into the dough, roll it out between sheets of wax paper. When the dough is rolled out, carefully lift off the paper.

To keep an unfilled crust from drying out, always cover it with plastic wrap while you're preparing the filling. If you prefer, you can place the crust in the refrigerator, but it still should be covered, as crusts can dry out in the refrigerator just as easily as on a countertop.

Really show-off crusts are easy to master. Just remember two things: First, make enough dough. A recipe for an 8-inch crust will fit in a 9-inch pie pan, but there won't be enough left over for an attractive fluted edge. The second secret is to lay the pastry evenly in the pan. An easy way to do this is simply to loosen the dough with a spatula, lay the pie pan upside down in the center of the rolled dough, gently lift the dough from underneath, and invert the pan. Another method is to wrap the dough loosely around the rolling pin and use the pin to lift the dough into the pan.

CRIMPING, FLUTING, AND DECORATING

In my recipes I have used "crimping" as the way to seal the edges of a double-crust pie and "fluting" as the way to decorate the edges of single-crust pies.

To crimp, trim the overhangs of both crusts to ¾ inch. Fold the overhangs under and press them together at regular intervals around the edge to form a tight seal.

Check your utensil drawer for some interesting crimping effects. Deeply patterned silverware handles, fork tines, even buttons can be pressed into pastry edges to make the crimping pretty.

To flute, trim the overhang to 1 inch and fold it under. Press the tip of your thumb and forefinger together on the inside edge of the crust, pinching the dough gently, and at the same time make an indentation with the tip of your other index finger on the outside edge. Repeat this pattern at intervals around the pan.

When crimping or fluting your pie crusts, make sure that the crust extends completely to the outer edge of the pie pan. This will cut down on possible shrinkage as it bakes.

You can cut decorative leaves, flowers, or other designs from pastry scraps. Attach them to the edge of the crust by moistening the surfaces with your fingertips; for an attractive glazed look, brush the decorations with beaten egg white.

BAKING

To prevent double-crust pies from leaking while they bake, you must make sure that the top crust is folded over the bottom crust and well sealed, and that you have cut adequate slits in the top crust to allow steam to escape. This makes for cleaner ovens as well as for attractive pies!

When baking filled single crusts, be sure to flute the edges high enough to incorporate the filling. Baked pie fillings, such as pumpkin and pecan, tend to expand somewhat, so be careful not to overfill the crusts or they will leak. Extra filling can always be baked in muffin tins or separate baking dishes.

Unless specifically called for in a recipe, don't put your pie pan on a baking sheet before placing it in the oven. This tends to disperse too much heat away from the bottom crust and can result in a soggy, unevenly baked pie.

Pies bake best on the bottom rack of the oven. Nearness to the heat source pre-

vents a soggy bottom crust. Also, the type of pie pan will affect how fast pastry bakes: heavier pans bake more slowly, as do shiny pans. Glass and aluminum pans bake more rapidly. So learn to rely on your eyes as well as your kitchen timer for perfect baking. When using glass or ceramic pie pans, be sure to reduce the oven temperature called for by 25°F (see page 11).

When baking pie crusts, check the pastry frequently as it bakes. Different cooks have different preferences for the "doneness" of their pastry. I favor a crisp crust that is deeply golden or browned around the edges, and my recipes give baking times with an eye to that result. Others like a moister crust baked only until it is lightly golden and may need to adjust the baking times listed here.

Some cooks prefer to prebake single crusts before filling them, particularly with slower-baking pies like custard or pecan. Preheat the oven to 425°F, and place the unbaked, unfilled crust on the bottom rack of the oven. Bake for 5 minutes. Remove from the oven, fill, and bake according to recipe directions.

How to tell if your fruit pie filling is done? Two ways: with a berry pie, the surest method is simply to look at it. If the filling is clearly bubbling through the slits in the top crust and the crust itself is evenly browned, the pie is done. Pies that contain sliced fruits (like peaches or apples) should be additionally tested with a fork or toothpick inserted through the slit into the fruit itself to ensure that the fruit is tender. If the crust

HOW TO EAT PASTRY SCRAPS

One of the great things about baking pies is that you usually wind up with pastry scraps—those delectable bits of dough left over from rolling and trimming your crust. The crust pastry recipes included here are generous in their proportions—partly so you will have some flexibility in the size of pie pan you can use and partly so you won't miss out on the joys of scraps.

The purists among you may maintain that the trimmings are best consumed raw—a practice dating from childhoods where snitching was part of the fun and a slap on the wrist pretty much went with the territory. Others, the gourmet school, will probably subscribe to more sophisticated methods of consumption: the scraps are adorned with bits of butter and sprinkles of cinnamon and sugar, or with jam, and then baked and eaten hot out of the oven.

The second practice has one important advantage over the first in that it generally ensures that your freshly baked pie will make it to dinnertime intact. Well-baked pastry scraps assuage the overwhelming impulse to break off a bit of crust "just for a taste."

Cinnamon Scraps: Place the pastry in a well-buttered baking pan. Dot generously with butter and sprinkle with cinnamon and sugar. Bake with the pie for 15 to 20 minutes.

Scrap Sandwiches: Roll the scraps together to a thickness of ⅛ inch. Cut the dough into strips approximately 1 x 2 inches, or use a small round biscuit cutter. Spread half the strips or rounds with raspberry or strawberry jam and place them on a well-buttered baking sheet. Top them with the remaining pieces and prick them with the tines of a fork. Bake with the pie for 20 to 25 minutes. Remove from the baking sheet and sprinkle with confectioners' sugar while still warm.

seems to be cooking too quickly for the fruit, lower the oven temperature to 350°F and continue baking until the fruit tests done.

FREEZING PASTRY CRUSTS

Many cooks like to make pie crust pastries in quantity and freeze them unbaked for future use. Be sure to choose a rich pastry recipe for freezing, one that uses approximately ⅓ cup shortening, butter, or lard for each 1¼ cups of flour. Pastry may either be rolled and shaped before freezing, or be frozen in balls and then thawed before rolling. (Of the crust recipes given here, only the Basic Crust, the Indestructible Crust, and the Meringue Crust do not freeze well.)

For unbaked shaped pie shells, freeze them first in their pie pans until solid. Remove them from the pans and stack them with layers of aluminum foil between for easy separation. Wrap the entire package in foil or seal it in a freezer bag. To use, place a frozen crust in a pie pan, prick it with the tines of a fork, and thaw it for 20 minutes before baking as usual.

Unless you have fantastic freezer space, it's nearly impossible to freeze top crusts flat. When preparing a two-crust pie from frozen dough, it is easier to invert a frozen shell over a thawed, filled bottom crust and allow it to thaw for 20 minutes. Crimp to seal the edges, cut slits in the top crust, and bake as usual.

Pastry balls can be frozen without rolling. Just wrap each one securely in foil or plastic wrap and seal it in a freezer bag. Frozen pastry balls should be thawed for 1 hour before rolling.

Baked pie shells are frozen with somewhat less success. Thawing can change the texture of a crust, and you run the risk of its becoming slightly soggy. If you do wish to freeze baked shells, be sure the crust is completely cooled before freezing, and wrap it securely. Do not unwrap before thawing.

Fruit pie fillings can be frozen, but they are best when frozen separately from the unbaked crusts. Prepare the fruit pie filling according to the recipe directions. Pour it into an *empty* pie pan and freeze it solid. Remove the frozen filling from the pie pan and wrap it securely in foil or plastic wrap, or seal it in a freezer bag. To thaw, unwrap the filling and place it in a prepared pastry shell. Thaw for 30 minutes at room temperature before baking as usual.

Cream pie fillings don't freeze well. They can turn grainy or spongy and will often separate in thawing. Don't try it.

BASIC PIE CRUST

2¼ cups all-purpose flour
1 teaspoon salt
⅔ cup shortening, chilled
4½ tablespoons ice water

1. Sift the flour and salt together in a large bowl. Cut in the shortening. With your fingertips, blend the flour and shortening together until the mixture has the texture of coarse crumbs.

2. Sprinkle the water evenly over the surface of the mixture. Blend only until all the ingredients are moistened and the dough can be shaped. Divide the dough into two equal portions and shape them into balls.

3. Place one portion on a lightly floured surface. Flatten it slightly and dust it with flour. Roll it out to a thickness of ⅛ inch, and ease it gently into a 9-inch pie pan. If you are making a double-crust pie, roll out the remaining dough to a thickness of $1/16$ inch and set it aside to be the top crust. If you are making single-crust pies, roll out the remaining dough to a thickness of ⅛ inch and use it for the second bottom crust.

4. To bake an unfilled pie crust, preheat the oven to 425° F. Prick the dough all over with the tines of a fork, and bake for 20 to 25 minutes, until the crust is golden.

Makes enough for 1 double-crust or 2 single-crust pies.

MAKE-AHEAD CRUST

This is a great all-purpose recipe for making pastry in quantity. The crusts can be made ahead and frozen, unbaked, or if the crusts are to be used within two weeks, they can be baked and then stored at room temperature in a tightly covered container, such as a large plastic storage box with a snap-on lid or a breadbox.

4½ cups all-purpose flour

2 teaspoons salt

⅓ cup lightly salted butter, chilled, cut into small pieces

⅓ cup lard, chilled

½ cup plus 2 tablespoons shortening, chilled

⅓ cup ice water

1. Sift the flour and salt together in a large bowl. Cut in the butter, lard, and shortening. Blend with your fingertips or a pastry blender until the mixture has the texture of coarse crumbs and will hold together when lightly pinched.

2. Sprinkle the water evenly over the surface of the mixture. Blend lightly, only until all the ingredients are moistened and the dough can be shaped. Divide the dough into four equal portions and shape them into balls.

3. Roll out each dough ball to a thickness of ⅛ inch and ease it gently into a pie pan. Flute the edges.

4. If you are freezing the crusts, place them unbaked in the freezer just until frozen, about 1 hour. Remove the crusts from the pans and stack them with a layer of aluminum foil separating each one. Wrap the package securely in foil and return it to the freezer until ready to use. Allow the crusts to thaw for 20 minutes before baking.

5. If you want to store baked crusts, prick the crusts all over with the tines of a fork and bake them for 20 to 25 minutes in a preheated 425° F oven, or until the crusts are lightly browned. Allow them to cool completely, then remove them from the pans. Wrap each one securely in aluminum foil and store them in a tightly covered container until ready to use.

Makes enough for four 9-inch pie crusts.

BUTTER CRUST

A tender, flaky pastry that is marvelously rich in both texture and flavor. A word of caution, though: This is a fragile crust that may be somewhat difficult for the beginner to handle. It helps to chill this dough for approximately 1 hour before rolling.

2¼ cups all-purpose flour

1 teaspoon salt

⅔ cup shortening, chilled

5 tablespoons lightly salted butter, chilled, cut into small pieces

5 tablespoons ice water

1. Sift the flour and salt together in a large bowl. Cut in the shortening and butter. Using your fingertips, blend the ingredients together until the mixture has the texture of coarse crumbs.

2. Sprinkle the water evenly over the mixture. Blend gently until all the ingredients are moistened and the dough can be shaped. Divide the dough into two equal portions and shape them into balls.

3. Place one portion on a lightly floured surface. Flatten it slightly and dust it with flour. Roll it out to a thickness of ⅛ inch, and ease it gently into a 9-inch pie pan. If you are making a double-crust pie, roll out the remaining dough to a thickness of ¹/₁₆ inch and set it aside to be the top crust. If you are making single-crust pies, roll out

> ### PIE FACT
> All the recipes here will fit standard-size pie pans, from 8 to 10 inches in diameter. Most of my recipes call for a 9-inch pan, but other sizes can be used. Just be prepared for leftover filling and pastry scraps when using 8-inch tins, or slightly less filling when using a 10-inch tin.

the remaining dough to a thickness of ⅛ inch and use it for the second bottom crust.

4. To bake an unfilled pie crust, preheat the oven to 425° F. Prick the dough all over with the tines of a fork, and bake for 20 to 25 minutes, until the crust is golden.

Makes enough for 1 double-crust or 2 single-crust pies.

MOM'S WHOLE-WHEAT PIE CRUST

My mother was something of a pioneer, advocating natural foods long before it became the trend. Keeping that in mind, she has provided her recipe for whole-wheat pie crust. I recommend it for its light nutty flavor and texture, as well as the added nutritional value of the whole grain flour. It's best with fruit fillings. You will note that whole-wheat pastry requires somewhat more water than other pastry recipes.

2 cups unbleached all-purpose white flour

1 cup whole-wheat flour

1½ teaspoons salt

8 tablespoons (½ cup) lightly salted butter, chilled, cut into small pieces

½ cup vegetable shortening, chilled

6 to 8 tablespoons ice water

1. Sift the flours and salt together in a large bowl. Cut in the butter and shortening, using your fingertips or a pastry blender, until the mixture has the texture of coarse crumbs.

2. Sprinkle the water over the crumb mixture, 1 tablespoon at a time, until the dough reaches the correct texture for shaping and rolling.

3. Divide the dough into two equal portions and shape them into balls. Place one portion on a lightly floured surface. Flatten it slightly and dust it with flour. Roll it out to a thickness of ⅛ inch and ease it gently into a 10-inch pie pan. If you are making a double-crust pie, roll out the remaining dough to a thickness of $1/16$ inch and set it aside to be the top crust. If you are making single-crust pies, roll out the remaining dough to a thickness of ⅛ inch and use it for a second bottom crust.

4. To bake an unfilled pie crust, preheat the oven to 425° F. Prick the dough all over with the tines of a fork, and bake for 20 to 25 minutes, until the crust is golden.

Makes enough for 1 double-crust or 2 single-crust pies.

INDESTRUCTIBLE CRUST

I guarantee that even the most inexperienced cook will not mess up this recipe. It's excellent with cream pies, or with any number of fruit pies.

2 cups all-purpose flour

10 tablespoons lightly salted butter, chilled, cut into small pieces

1 egg yolk, lightly beaten

5 to 6 tablespoons ice water

1. Place the flour in a large bowl and cut in the butter, blending with your fingertips or a pastry blender until the mixture has the texture of coarse crumbs.

2. Make a well in the center of the mixture and add the egg yolk and 5 tablespoons water. Working from the sides, gradually incorporate the flour until the dough forms a rough mass. Add more water only if necessary. Divide the dough into two equal portions and shape them into balls.

3. Place one portion on a lightly floured surface. Flatten it slightly and dust it with flour. Roll it out to a thickness of ⅛ inch, and ease it gently into a 9-inch pie pan. If you are making a double-crust pie, roll out the remaining dough to a thickness of $1/16$

PIE FACT

Baking for a crowd? Almost any pie recipe can be adapted to make a pan pie (see pages 84, 86). Filling recipes should be doubled to fit the larger, rectangular pans, as should cookie-crumb crust recipes. Pastry crust recipes needn't be increased, just rolled out to fit the pan.

---

inch and set it aside to be the top crust. If you are making single-crust pies, roll out the remaining dough to a thickness of ⅛ inch and use it for the second bottom crust.

4. To bake an unfilled pie crust, preheat the oven to 425° F. Prick the dough all over with the tines of a fork, and bake for 20 to 25 minutes, until the crust is golden.

Makes enough for 1 double-crust or 2 single-crust pies.

OLD-FASHIONED LARD CRUST

2¼ cups all-purpose flour
1 teaspoon salt
⅓ cup lard, chilled
½ cup shortening, chilled
4 to 5 tablespoons ice water

1. Sift the flour together with the salt in a large bowl. Cut in the lard and shortening. Work with your fingertips or a pastry blender until the mixture has the texture of coarse crumbs. When the mixture is properly blended, the crumbs will hold together with a light pinch. Sprinkle 4 tablespoons water over the surface of the mixture; blend with your fingertips only until all the ingredients are moistened and can be shaped into a ball. Add the additional tablespoon of water only if necessary. Divide the dough into two equal portions and shape them into balls.

2. Place one portion of the dough on a lightly floured surface. Flatten it slightly and dust it with flour. Roll it out to a thickness of ⅛ inch, and ease it gently into a 10-inch pie pan. If you are making a double-crust pie, roll out the remaining dough to a thickness of $1/16$ inch and set it aside to be the top crust. If you are making single-crust pies, roll out the remaining dough to a thickness of ⅛ inch and use it for the second bottom crust.

3. To bake an unfilled pie crust, preheat the oven to 425° F. Prick the dough all over with the tines of a fork, and bake for 20 to 25 minutes, until the crust is golden.

Makes enough for 1 double-crust or 2 single-crust pies.

LATTICE TOP CRUST

1. Roll out ½ recipe of any of the double-crust recipes (except the Butter Crust, which is too soft) to a thickness of ⅛ inch. Cut the dough into strips ¾ inch wide. You should have about 12 strips.

2. Lay 5 to 6 strips, evenly spaced, over a filled crust; attach each at one end by moistening your fingertips slightly and pressing them into the pie edge. These will be your lengthwise strips.

3. Gently roll up 5 to 6 remaining strips. These will be used to weave across the pie, over and under the attached lengthwise strips. Attach the first of these weaving strips to the edge of the pie pan, about 1½ inches from the first lengthwise strip.

4. Unroll about 1 inch of the strip and pass it over the first lengthwise strip. Unroll a little more and slip it under the second lengthwise strip. Continue this over/under pattern, unrolling just as much of the strip as you need, until you reach the opposite edge of the pie.

5. Attach a second rolled strip 1 inch from the first. Gently lift the first lengthwise strip and unroll enough of the weaving strip to slip under. Then, unroll enough to pass over the next lengthwise strip. Continue across, reversing the over/under pattern of the first weaving strip. Continue weaving the remaining rolled strips in the over/under pattern.

6. Trim the strips to a 1-inch overhang. Fold the bottom crust over the strip edges and crimp to seal.

7. Before baking (in a preheated 400°F oven), cut a 2-inch strip of aluminum foil and fold it loosely around the pie edge.

PECAN CRUST

The crunchiness of this pastry provides a perfect complement to a cool, smooth filling such as the one called for in the Black Magic Pie on page 75.

2¼ cups all-purpose flour
½ cup ground pecans (about ¼ pound)
1 teaspoon salt
1 tablespoon sugar
⅔ cup butter-flavored shortening
4 tablespoons ice water

1. Sift the dry ingredients together in a large bowl and toss to blend.

2. Add the shortening and lightly blend, using your fingertips, until the mixture has the texture of coarse crumbs. Sprinkle the water evenly over the flour mixture, 1 tablespoon at a time. Gently blend until the ingredients are moistened and the dough can be shaped. Divide the dough into two equal portions, shape them into balls, wrap each in plastic wrap or wax paper, and chill.

3. Preheat the oven to 425°F.

4. Place one portion of the dough on a lightly floured surface. Flatten it slightly and dust it with flour. Roll it out to a thickness of ¼ inch and ease it gently into a 9-inch pie pan. Repeat this with the second portion. Flute the edges as desired. Prick the dough all over with the tines of a fork, and bake for 20 to 25 minutes, or until the crust is golden.

Makes enough for 2 single-crust pies.

GRAHAM CRACKER CRUST

1½ cups graham cracker crumbs (about 20 crackers)

5 tablespoons butter, melted

¼ cup sugar

1. Set aside 4 tablespoons of the crumbs for garnish.

2. In a medium-size bowl, combine the remaining crumbs, the butter, and the sugar. Blend well. Press the mixture into a 9-inch pie pan, covering the bottom and the sides evenly. Chill.

Makes enough for 1 single-crust pie.

GINGERSNAP CRUST

1½ cups gingersnap cookie crumbs (approximately 8 ounces gingersnap cookies)

½ teaspoon ground ginger

5 tablespoons lightly salted butter, melted

1. Set aside 2 tablespoons of the crumbs for garnish.

2. In a medium-size bowl, combine the remaining crumbs with the ground ginger, and toss to blend.

3. Add the butter and mix well. Press the mixture into the bottom and sides of a 9-inch pie pan. Chill.

Makes enough for 1 single-crust pie.

OREO COOKIE CRUST

2½ cups (about ¾ pound) crushed Oreo or other chocolate sandwich cookies (with vanilla or chocolate filling)

2½ tablespoons lightly salted butter, melted

1. Set aside ¼ cup crumbs for garnish.

2. In a medium-size bowl, thoroughly blend the remaining cookie crumbs with the butter. Press the mixture into the bottom and sides of a 9-inch pie pan. Chill.

Makes enough for 1 single-crust pie.

MERINGUE CRUST

Great for cream-type pie fillings, including Renata's Angel Pie (see page 65) and Chocolate Cream Pie (see page 76), or any of the cooked lemon or lime fillings. For a light dessert, try Strawberry-Banana Yogurt filling (see page 68) or simply fill a cooled crust with softened vanilla ice cream and top with sliced fresh fruit.

4 egg whites, at room temperature

1 cup sugar

½ cup shredded coconut (optional)

1. Preheat the oven to 250° F.

2. Beat the egg whites until stiff but not dry. Gradually add the sugar, beating constantly until the mixture is thick, glossy, and stands in stiff peaks.

3. Turn the meringue into a well-buttered 10-inch pie pan. Spread it evenly over the bottom and bring it up in evenly spaced peaks around the sides. If desired, sprinkle with coconut.

4. Bake for 1 hour. Turn the oven off but leave the crust in it until the oven is cold.

Makes enough for 1 single-crust pie.

THE WELL-FILLED PIE

FRUIT PIES
CREAM AND CUSTARD PIES
NUT AND CHOCOLATE PIES
OLD-FASHIONED PIES

MOM'S APPLE PIE

No, this isn't my mother's recipe for apple pie—but she does agree that it's the best she ever tasted, so I decided to name it after her anyway.

1 recipe Basic Pie Crust (see page 25),
    Butter Crust (see page 27), or Mom's
    Whole-Wheat Pie Crust (see page 28)

1 cup sugar

2 tablespoons all-purpose flour

2 generous teaspoons ground cinnamon

¾ teaspoon ground nutmeg

3½ cups peeled, cored, and sliced
    McIntosh apples (about 4 to 5 apples)

3 cups peeled, cored, and sliced Granny
    Smith apples (about 4 apples)

2 tablespooons lightly salted butter

½ cup heavy or whipping cream

1. Prepare the Basic, Butter, or Whole-Wheat Pie Crust dough and divide it into two equal portions. On a lightly floured surface, roll out half the dough to a thickness of ⅛ inch. Ease it gently into a 9-inch pie pan; trim the overhang to ¾ inch. Set it aside. Roll out the remaining dough to a thickness of 1/16 inch and set it aside.

2. Preheat the oven to 400° F.

3. Combine the sugar, flour, and spices in a large bowl. Add the apple slices and toss until they are well coated. Fill the crust with the apple slices and dot them with the butter. Ease the top crust over the filled bottom crust; trim the overhang to ¾ inch. Fold the top crust over the bottom. Crimp to seal the edges. Cut slits in the top crust to allow steam to escape.

4. Bake for 1 hour, or until the crust is golden and the apples test done.

5. Turn off the oven and remove the pie. Gently pour the cream through the slits in the crust. Return the pie to the oven and leave it there until the oven is nearly cool, about 20 minutes. Serve immediately.

PIE FACT

According to the *Guinness Book of World Records,* the largest apple pie ever baked was at the Orleans County fair in New York in August of 1977. Resident bakers used a baking dish 16½ feet in diameter, 300 bushels of apples, and 5,950 pounds of sugar. The total weight of the pie was 21,210 pounds.

APPLE PIE WITH WHITE WINE

A great recipe for less than perfect apples—the wine adds a hint of tartness and really livens up the fruit.

1 recipe Indestructible Crust (see page 29) or Basic Pie Crust (see page 25)

⅔ cup sugar

1½ teaspoons ground cinnamon

½ teaspoon ground nutmeg

¼ cup all-purpose flour

5 cups peeled, cored, and sliced tart apples (5 to 6 apples)

2 tablespoons lightly salted butter

⅓ cup plus 3 tablespoons white wine

1. Prepare the Indestructible or Basic Pie Crust dough and divide it in half. Roll out half the dough on a lightly floured surface to a thickness of ⅛ inch. Ease it gently into a 9-inch pie pan; trim the overhang to ¾ inch. Set it aside. Roll out the remaining dough to a thickness of ¹/₁₆ inch, and set it aside.

2. Preheat the oven to 400° F.

3. In a large bowl, combine the sugar, spices, and flour. Add the apple slices and toss until they are well coated.

4. Place the apple slices in the crust. Dot with the butter, and pour the wine over all.

5. Ease the top crust over the filled bottom crust; trim the overhang to ¾ inch. Fold the top crust over the bottom. Crimp to seal the edges. Cut slits in the top crust to allow steam to escape.

6. Bake for 1 hour, or until the crust is lightly browned and the apples test done.

CHARLIE'S BLUEBERRY PIE

Charlie, my father, travels a good deal and maintains that blueberry pie is a sure bet in almost any restaurant in the country. Though he's not much of a baker, Dad does have a definite feeling about the perfect blueberry pie—not overly sweet, a hint of lemon for tartness, and a slightly runny filling. The following recipe meets all those requirements.

1 recipe Mom's Whole-Wheat Pie Crust (see page 28) or Basic Pie Crust (see page 25)

3 cups fresh blueberries

¾ cup sugar

1 tablespoon freshly grated lemon peel

1 tablespoon freshly squeezed lemon juice

3 tablespoons minute or instant tapioca

2 tablespoons lightly salted butter

1. Prepare the Whole-Wheat or Basic Pie Crust dough and divide it into two equal portions. Roll out half the dough to a thickness of ⅛ inch. Ease it into a 9-inch pie pan and trim the overhang to ¾ inch. Set it aside. Roll out the remaining dough to a thickness of 1/16 inch and set it aside.

2. Preheat the oven to 400° F.

3. Wash, drain, and sort the berries; toss them together with the sugar, lemon peel, lemon juice, and tapioca. Allow to stand 15 minutes.

4. Turn the berry mixture into the crust; dot with the butter.

5. Ease the top crust over the filled bottom crust; trim the overhang to ¾ inch. Fold the top crust over the bottom. Crimp to seal the edges. Cut slits in the top crust to allow steam to escape

6. Bake for 50 to 60 minutes, or until the crust is golden.

FRESH STRAWBERRY PIE

Fresh berries that are rolled in sugar and arranged in the crust before filling make this one of the most attractive and freshest-tasting berry pies.

½ recipe Basic Pie Crust (see page 25)
2 pints (4 cups) ripe strawberries, washed and hulled
1 cup granulated sugar
½ cup water
4 tablespoons cornstarch
2 tablespoons lightly salted butter
Approximately ½ cup confectioners' sugar
Unsweetened Whipped Cream (see page 73)

1. Preheat the oven to 425° F.

2. Prepare the Basic Pie Crust dough and roll it out on a lightly floured surface to a thickness of ⅛ inch. Ease it gently into a 9-inch pie pan; trim the overhang to 1 inch and flute the edges as desired. Prick the crust all over with the tines of a fork and bake for 20 to 25 minutes, or until the crust is golden. Set it aside to cool.

3. Purée 1 pint of the berries in the workbowl of a blender or food processor to make approximately 1 cup. Combine the puréed berries with the granulated sugar, water, and cornstarch in a medium saucepan.

4. Cook over medium heat, stirring constantly, until the mixture is quite thick and mounds slightly when dropped from a spoon. Add the butter and stir constantly until it has melted. Remove from the heat and cool slightly.

5. Roll the remaining berries in the confectioners' sugar and arrange them in the crust, pointed side up.

6. Pour the cooked filling over the berries and allow it to remain at room temperature or in the refrigerator until set. Serve topped with Unsweetened Whipped Cream, if desired.

FLAVORED WHIPPED CREAM

Try experimenting with different liqueurs to flavor a whipped cream topping for your pies. Use crème de cassis–flavored cream, for example, over blueberry pie, Calvados cream over apple pie, grenadine over cherry. The possibilities are endless! Whip in 2 tablespoons liqueur to 1 cup sweetened or unsweetened whipped cream; drizzle a little extra liqueur over the top to serve.

SPRINGTIME STRAWBERRY-RHUBARB PIE

A great combination of flavors...

½ recipe Butter Crust (see page 27)

2 cups sliced fresh rhubarb (about 4 large stalks)

1¼ cups sugar

1⅓ cups cold water

3½ tablespoons cornstarch

2 cups sliced ripe strawberries, washed and hulled first

4 to 5 drops red food coloring (optional)

Whole strawberries for garnish

Make-Ahead Whipped Cream (recipe follows)

GREAT FRUIT PIE COMBINATIONS

Apple/Blackberry
Blueberry/Cranberry
Cranberry/Apple
Mulberry/Rhubarb
Strawberry/Peach
Peach/Damson Plum
Kiwi/Apple, Peach, or Strawberry

1. Preheat the oven to 425° F.

2. Prepare the Butter Crust dough and roll it out on a lightly floured surface to a thickness of ⅛ inch. Ease it gently into a 9-inch pie pan, and trim the overhang to 1 inch. Flute the edges as desired. Prick the crust all over with the tines of a fork, and bake for 20 to 25 minutes, or until the crust is golden. Set it aside to cool.

3. Place the rhubarb, sugar, and 1 cup of the water in a medium-size saucepan. Bring to a boil over medium heat, stirring until the sugar dissolves. Reduce the heat, and stew the rhubarb until almost tender, about 5 minutes.

4. Dissolve the cornstarch in the remaining ⅓ cup cold water and set it aside.

5. Add the strawberries to the rhubarb mixture and cook just until the rhubarb and berries are tender, about 3 minutes.

6. Add a small amount of hot liquid from the saucepan to the cornstarch mixture and stir it well. Add the cornstarch to the saucepan. Blend thoroughly and continue cooking over low heat for 6 to 7 minutes, stirring constantly, until the mixture is no longer cloudy and is sufficiently thickened. Remove from the heat, and add food coloring if desired.

7. Pour the mixture into the crust. Allow the pie to stand for several hours before serving, or chill it before serving if preferred. Serve garnished with whole strawberries and topped with Make-Ahead Whipped Cream.

MAKE-AHEAD WHIPPED CREAM

This recipe for whipped cream has a couple of advantages: it's not as sweet as some creams, and the addition of corn syrup as a sweetener stabilizes the whipped cream somewhat, so that it can be made as much as 2 hours before serving.

1 cup heavy or whipping cream, chilled

½ teaspoon vanilla extract

2 tablespoons light corn syrup

Thoroughly chill the mixing bowl and beaters of an electric mixer. Whip the cream in the bowl until soft peaks form. Continue beating; add the vanilla, and then add the syrup in a thin stream, and beat until the mixture stands in soft peaks. If prepared much before serving time, whisk again lightly before serving.

BLUEBERRY-PEACH PIE

Mixed fruit pies are always great favorites. This is one of the best—wonderful to look at and wonderful to eat!

1 recipe Butter Crust (see page 27) or
  Mom's Whole-Wheat Pie Crust (see
  page 28)
4 fresh peaches (about 1 pound)
2 cups fresh blueberries
⅔ cup sugar
3½ tablespoons minute or instant tapioca
2 tablespoons lightly salted butter

1. Prepare the Butter or Whole-Wheat Pie Crust dough and divide it into two equal portions. On a lightly floured surface, roll out half the dough to a thickness of ⅛ inch. Ease it into a 9-inch pie pan and trim the overhang to ¾ inch. Set it aside. Roll out the remaining dough to a thickness of ¹/₁₆ inch and set it aside.

2. Preheat the oven to 400° F.

3. Peel, pit, and cut the peaches into slices about ½ inch thick. Wash, drain, and sort the blueberries.

4. In a large bowl, toss the fruit together with the sugar and tapioca until well coated. Allow to stand at room temperature for 15 minutes. Turn the fruit into the crust; dot with the butter.

5. Ease the top crust over the filled bottom crust; trim the overhang to ¾ inch. Fold the top crust over the bottom. Crimp to seal the edges. Cut slits in the top crust to allow steam to escape.

6. Bake for 50 to 60 minutes, or until the crust is golden and the fruit tests done.

STREUSEL CRUMB TOPPING FOR FRUIT PIES

Variously referred to as German, Dutch, and French, crumb topping is a great substitute for a top crust on any kind of fruit pie. Combine ¾ cup all-purpose flour, ½ cup sugar, and ½ cup lightly salted butter until the mixture has the texture of coarse crumbs. Sprinkle evenly over an unbaked filled crust and bake as usual.

SOUR CHERRY PIE

*1 recipe Butter Crust (see page 27) or
Basic Pie Crust (see page 25)*

*1¼ cups sugar for fresh cherries, 1⅓ cups
for canned cherries*

5 tablespoons all-purpose flour

*4 cups fresh sour cherries, stems removed,
pitted, or 3 cups canned drained tart
cherries (reserve the liquid)*

*¼ cup water, or ½ cup liquid from canned
cherries*

*½ teaspoon almond extract (optional for
fresh cherries)*

¼ teaspoon red food coloring (optional)

2 tablespoons lightly salted butter

Sweetened Sour Cream (recipe follows)

1. Prepare the Butter or Basic Pie Crust dough and divide it into two equal portions. On a lightly floured surface roll out half the dough to a thickness of ⅛ inch. Ease it gently into a 9-inch pie pan; trim the overhang to 1 inch. Roll out the remaining dough to a thickness of ⅛ inch and cut it into strips ¾ inch wide. Cover the strips loosely with plastic wrap while the filling is being prepared.

2. Preheat the oven to 400° F.

3. In a large bowl, sift together the sugar and flour. Add the cherries, water or cherry liquid, almond extract (if needed), and food coloring if desired; allow to stand for 20 minutes.

4. Pour the filling into the crust and dot with the butter. Top with a Lattice Top Crust (see page 31); trim the overhang to 1 inch. Fold the bottom crust over the strip edges to seal. Crimp the edges to seal. Cut a 2-inch strip of aluminum foil and fold loosely around the pie edge.

5. Bake for 40 minutes; remove the foil and continue baking an additional 10 minutes. To serve, top with Sweetened Sour Cream.

SWEETENED SOUR CREAM

1 cup sour cream

3 tablespoons confectioners' sugar

Combine the sour cream and confectioners' sugar and stir until well blended. Spoon over cooled pie wedges to serve.

PIE FACT

Always taste the fruit before sweetening fruit pies. If it seems very sour, add a pinch of salt. The salt will counteract the need for additional sugar in the recipe.

BLACKBERRY PIE

Depending on where you live, you may call any of three different kinds of fruit blackberries. In the north and the midwest, the large oblong berries called blackberries are actually loganberries and make for a wonderfully flavorful pie. In urban areas, it is often the black raspberry that is sold under the name of blackberry. A small, round berry that is very black when ripe is the true blackberry, and it is almost always found growing wild as it resists cultivation. These berries require the addition of a hint of lemon juice to liven up their flavor, as well as water to augment their juice. Whatever variety you have on hand, this recipe will make for a great pie; just make the few adjustments called for.

1 recipe Butter Crust (see page 27) or
Basic Pie Crust (see page 25)

4 cups blackberries

1 cup sugar

3½ tablespoons minute or instant tapioca

½ teaspoon ground dried orange peel

2 tablespoons lightly salted butter

IF USING WILD BLACKBERRIES ADD:

2 tablespoons freshly squeezed lemon juice

¼ cup cold water

1. Prepare the Butter or Basic Pie Crust dough and divide it in half. On a lightly floured surface, roll out half the dough to a thickness of ⅛ inch. Ease it gently into a 9-inch pie pan; trim the overhang to ¾ inch. Set it aside. Roll out the remaining dough to a thickness of ¹/₁₆ inch and set it aside.

2. Preheat the oven to 425° F.

3. In a medium-size bowl, combine the berries, sugar, tapioca, and orange peel and toss. Add the lemon juice and water if necessary. Allow the mixture to stand for 15 minutes.

4. Turn the berry mixture into the crust, and dot with the butter.

5. Ease the top crust over the filled bottom crust; trim the overhang to ¾ inch. Fold the top crust over the bottom. Crimp to seal the edges. Cut slits in the top crust to allow steam to escape.

6. Bake for 15 minutes. Reduce the heat to 375° F and bake for an additional 30 to 35 minutes, or until the crust is lightly browned and the filling is bubbly. Set the pie aside for 30 minutes before serving. Top with vanilla ice cream if desired.

MULBERRY PIE

My mother's backyard abounds with mulberry trees. As children, we harvested them the quickest and easiest way possible—a clean cloth laid under the tree and a good shake to the trunk. Mother's word of advice for Mulberry Pie: The berries require less sugar as the season progresses; taste your berries first. If they seem very sweet, the sugar here can be cut by as much as ¼ cup.

1 recipe Basic Pie Crust (see page 25) or
   Butter Crust (see page 27)

4 cups mulberries

1 cup sugar

5 tablespoons all-purpose flour

2 tablespoons freshly squeezed lemon juice

1 teaspoon freshly grated lemon peel

2 tablespoons lightly salted butter

Nutmeg Whipped Cream (recipe follows)

1. Prepare the Basic or Butter Crust dough and divide it in half. On a lightly floured surface, roll out half the dough to a thickness of ⅛ inch. Ease it gently into a 9-inch pie pan; trim the overhang to ¾ inch. Set it aside. Roll out the remaining dough to a thickness of 1/16 inch and set it aside, or cut it into strips for lattice crust if preferred (see page 31).

2. Preheat the oven to 400° F.

3. In a large bowl, combine the berries, sugar, flour, lemon juice, and lemon peel.

Toss well and allow the mixture to stand for 20 minutes.

4. Turn the berry mixture into the crust; dot with the butter. Ease the top crust over the filled bottom crust; trim the overhang to ¾ inch. Fold the top crust over the bottom. Crimp to seal the edges. Cut slits in the top crust to allow steam to escape.

5. Bake for 45 to 50 minutes, or until the crust is lightly browned and the filling is bubbly. Top with Nutmeg Whipped Cream.

NUTMEG WHIPPED CREAM

2 cups heavy or whipping cream

4 tablespoons sugar

½ teaspoon ground nutmeg

Thoroughly chill the mixing bowl and beaters of an electric mixer. Whip the cream in the bowl until soft peaks form. Gradually add the sugar and continue beating until well blended. Stir in the nutmeg to blend, and sprinkle with extra nutmeg, if desired.

GOOSEBERRY MERINGUE

If you're using fresh gooseberries, make sure they're really ripe. In addition to their natural pale green, ripe gooseberries have a slight orchid tinge.

½ recipe Butter Crust (see page 27), or 1 baked Make-Ahead Crust (see page 26)

2 cups fresh gooseberries, washed and sorted, or 2 cups canned berries, drained (reserve the liquid)

½ cup water, or ½ cup liquid from canned berries

¼ cup all-purpose flour

1⅓ cups sugar for fresh berries, 1 cup for canned berries

⅛ teaspoon salt

Meringue (recipe follows)

1. If you are using the Butter Crust, preheat the oven to 425° F. Prepare the dough and roll it out on a lightly floured surface to a thickness of ⅛ inch. Ease it gently into an 8-inch pie pan; trim the overhang to 1 inch. Flute the edges as desired. Prick the crust all over with the tines of a fork, and bake for 20 to 25 minutes, or until the crust is golden. Set it aside to cool.

If you are using the Make-Ahead Crust, place it in a pie pan and allow it to defrost. Preheat the oven to 425° F.

2. Combine the berries and water or berry liquid in a medium saucepan. Stew the fresh berries over medium heat until tender. If using canned berries, cook only until heated through.

3. Sift together the flour, sugar, and salt; add to the berries and stir until the sugar dissolves. Cook, stirring constantly, until the mixture is thick and will mound slightly when dropped from a spoon, about 5 minutes.

4. Pour the mixture into the crust. Spread the meringue evenly over the filling so that none shows through, being careful to seal the edges.

5. Bake for 12 to 15 minutes, or until the meringue is lightly browned. Allow the pie to stand at room temperature until the filling is set, then refrigerate.

MERINGUE

2 egg whites, at room temperature

5 tablespoons sugar

In a medium-size bowl, beat the egg whites until stiff but not dry. Gradually add the sugar, 1 tablespoon at a time, beating constantly until the mixture is thick, glossy, and stands in stiff peaks.

PIE FACT

Those in the know practice from two to three months before entering a pie-eating contest. The experts say that any and all practice sessions should involve increasing the rate of pie consumption, rather than increasing the quantities of pies consumed. Most competitive pie eaters prefer fruit pies to gooier nut or meringue pies, which tend to slow them down.

MIXED FRUIT PIE

Here is an all-purpose recipe for fruit pie. I have made some suggestions for great combinations (see page 42), but don't be afraid to experiment with the fruits you have on hand for some delicious special effects. Remember to taste your fruit—tart fruits like apples, peaches, or cranberries require more sugar than do sweet fruits like berries or plums. If you are using the Basic or Indestructible Crust, you may wish to try a lattice top (see page 31).

1 recipe Butter Crust (see page 27), Basic Pie Crust (see page 25), or Indestructible Crust (see page 29)

Mixed fresh fruit, washed, peeled, sliced, and pitted as necessary, to make 5½ to 6 cups

¾ to 1 cup sugar

¼ cup all-purpose flour, or 4 tablespoons minute or instant tapioca

1 tablespoon freshly squeezed lemon juice

2 tablespoons lightly salted butter

¼ cup light cream or half-and-half

1. Prepare the Butter, Basic, or Indestructible Crust dough and divide it in half. On a lightly floured surface, roll out half the dough to a thickness of ⅛ inch. Ease it gently into a 9-inch pie pan; trim the overhang to ¾ inch. Set it aside. Roll out the remaining dough to a thickness of 1/16 inch and set it aside.

2. Preheat the oven to 400° F.

3. In a large bowl, combine the fruits with the sugar, flour or tapioca, and lemon juice, and toss until well coated. Allow to stand 15 minutes.

4. Turn the fruit mixture into the crust; dot with the butter, and pour the cream over all.

5. Ease the top crust over the filled bottom crust; trim the overhang to ¾ inch. Fold the top crust over the bottom. Crimp to seal the edges. Cut slits in the top crust to allow steam to escape. Bake for 45 to 50 minutes, or until the crust is lightly browned, the filling is bubbly, and the fruit tests done.

NATURAL KEY LIME PIE

The natural pale yellow-green of this filling is infinitely more appealing to eye and palate than its bright green counterpart tinted with food coloring. For added appeal, sprinkle a touch of freshly grated lime peel over the baked meringue.

½ recipe Butter Crust (see page 27)

1 cup sugar

1¼ cups cold water

2 tablespoons lightly salted butter

¼ cup cornstarch

Grated peel of 4 Key limes or 3 regular limes (about 3½ tablespoons)

Juice from 3 Key limes or 2 regular limes (about ½ cup)

3 eggs, at room temperature, separated

2 tablespoons milk

Meringue (recipe follows)

1. Preheat the oven to 425° F.

2. Prepare the Butter Crust dough and roll it out to a thickness of ⅛ inch. Ease it into a 9-inch pie pan and trim the overhang to 1 inch. Flute the edges as desired. Prick the crust all over with the tines of a fork and bake for 20 to 25 minutes, or until the crust is golden. Set it aside to cool. Don't turn off the oven.

3. Combine the sugar, 1 cup of the water, and the butter in the top of a double boiler and heat over boiling water until the mixture is steaming (not quite boiling).

4. In a small bowl, combine the cornstarch and remaining cold water to make a paste, and add this to the sugar mixture.

5. Add 2½ tablespoons of the lime peel and all the lime juice to the sugar mixture and cook, stirring constantly, until the mixture is thick and mounds slightly when dropped from a spoon.

6. In a medium-size bowl, beat the egg yolks together with the milk. (Reserve the whites for the meringue.) Add a small amount of the hot mixture to the egg yolks and blend. Add the yolks to the saucepan and cook, stirring constantly, until the mixture has thickened and has lost any eggy taste, about 5 minutes. Remove from the heat, cool slightly, and pour into the crust. Spread the meringue evenly over the filling so that none shows through, being careful to seal the edges.

7. Bake for 12 to 15 minutes, or until the meringue is lightly browned. Allow the pie to stand at room temperature until the filling is set, then refrigerate. Sprinkle with the remaining lime peel before serving.

MERINGUE

3 egg whites, at room temperature

6 tablespoons sugar

In a medium-size bowl, beat the egg whites until stiff but not dry. Continue beating and add the sugar 1 tablespoon at a time. Beat until the mixture is thick, glossy, and stands in stiff peaks.

SUNDAY DINNER LEMON MERINGUE

I'll bet my mom's lemon pie—so tart and fresh tasting—can beat your mom's lemon pie any day. If you don't believe me, just give it a try.

½ recipe Butter Crust (see page 27)

1 cup sugar

1¼ cups water

1 tablespoon lightly salted butter

½ cup plus 2 tablespoons lemon juice
  (about 3 large lemons)

2 tablespoons freshly grated lemon peel
  (about 1 large lemon)

Scant ¼ cup cornstarch

4 tablespoons cold water

3 eggs, at room temperature, separated

2 tablespoons milk

Meringue (recipe follows)

1. Preheat the oven to 425° F.

2. Prepare the Butter Crust dough and roll it out on a lightly floured surface to a thickness of ⅛ inch. Ease it gently into a 9-inch pie pan; trim the overhang to 1 inch. Flute the edges as desired. Prick the crust all over with the tines of a fork. Bake for 20 to 25 minutes, or until the crust is golden. Set it aside to cool. Don't turn off the oven.

3. Place the sugar and water in the top of a double boiler set over boiling water and stir until the sugar dissolves. Add the butter, and stir until it has melted.

4. Add the lemon juice and peel and blend well. Dissolve the cornstarch in the cold water and add this to the lemon juice mixture. Stir to blend. Continue cooking, stirring constantly, until the mixture is thick enough to coat a spoon. (If you are unsure about the thickness, taste the mixture. It should taste like lemon, not like starch.)

5. In a small bowl, beat the egg yolks with the milk. (Reserve the whites for the meringue.) Add a small amount of the hot mixture to the egg yolks and blend. Add the yolks to the saucepan and continue to cook, stirring constantly, until the mixture is once again thick enough to coat a spoon, 8 to 10 minutes. Remove it from the heat and allow it to cool slightly. Pour the filling into the crust. Spread the meringue over the cooled filling so that none shows through, being careful to seal the edges.

6. Bake for 20 minutes, or until the meringue is lightly browned. Allow the pie to stand at room temperature until the filling is set, then refrigerate.

MERINGUE

3 egg whites, at room temperature

6 tablespoons sugar

1 tablespoon freshly squeezed lemon juice

1. In a medium-size bowl, beat the egg whites until stiff but not dry. Continue beating and add the sugar, 1 tablespoon at a time. Beat until the mixture is thick, glossy, and stands in stiff peaks.

2. Add the lemon juice and beat well.

LOUISIANA LEMONADE PIE

For a cook in a rush, a lemon pie like this can be the answer. The gingersnap crust provides a nice complement to the sweetness of the filling. Be sure to use a brand of whipped topping that contains real cream, and the results will be difficult to distinguish from a pie that took hours to make!

1 recipe Gingersnap Crust (see page 33)
1 8-ounce carton frozen whipped topping
1 6-ounce can frozen lemonade
    concentrate
2 tablespoons freshly squeezed lemon juice
2 teaspoons freshly grated lemon peel
1 14-ounce can sweetened condensed milk

1. Prepare the Gingersnap Crust, reserving 2 tablespoons crumbs for garnish. Set it aside.

2. Without thawing the topping or the lemonade, put all the remaining ingredients in a large bowl.

3. Beat with an electric mixer at low speed until thoroughly combined. Switch the mixer speed to high and continue beating for 3 minutes.

4. Pour the filling into the crust and garnish with the reserved crumbs. Chill for several hours before serving, or freeze if desired.

BUTTERSCOTCH PEACH PIE

Like penicillin, this recipe was invented by accident. I ran out of granulated sugar one day and decided to experiment with brown sugar instead. The result is a fabulous combination of flavors.

1 recipe Basic Pie Crust (see page 25)

5 cups peeled and sliced fresh peaches (about 1½ pounds; see Note)

1¼ cups light brown sugar, firmly packed

3½ tablespoons all-purpose flour

2 tablespoons lightly salted butter

3 tablespoons milk

1. Prepare the Basic Pie Crust dough and divide it into two equal portions. On a lightly floured surface, roll out half the dough to a thickness of ⅛ inch. Ease it gently into a 9-inch pie pan; trim the overhang to ¾ inch. Set it aside. Roll out the remaining dough to a thickness of 1/16 inch and set it aside.

2. Preheat the oven to 400° F.

3. Place the peaches in a large bowl; add the brown sugar and flour and toss until well coated.

4. Place the fruit and sugar mixture in the crust. Dot with the butter and sprinkle the milk evenly over the fruit.

5. Ease the top crust over the filled bottom crust; trim the overhang to ¾ inch. Fold the top crust over the bottom. Crimp to seal the edges. Cut slits in the top crust to allow steam to escape.

6. Bake for 50 minutes, or until the crust is evenly browned and the fruit is tender.

Note: Peaches peel easily after being submerged in boiling water for 2 to 3 minutes.

JESSIE LOU'S FAVORITE: PINEAPPLE MERINGUE

This one gets my grandmother's vote for the American Pie Hall of Fame—creamy pineapple custard topped with an airy meringue. Perfect.

½ recipe Butter Crust (see page 27)

4 tablespoons sugar

3½ tablespoons cornstarch

2 cups milk

1 small can (8 ounces) unsweetened chopped pineapple, undrained, or 1 cup chopped fresh pineapple, including juice

3 eggs, at room temperature, separated

1 teaspoon vanilla extract

Meringue (recipe follows)

1. Preheat the oven to 425° F.

2. Prepare the Butter Crust dough and roll it out on a lightly floured surface to a thickness of ⅛ inch. Ease it gently into a 9-inch pie pan; trim the overhang to 1 inch and crimp the edges as desired. Prick the crust all over with the tines of a fork and bake for 20 to 25 minutes, or until the crust is golden. Set it aside to cool. Don't turn off the oven.

3. In a medium-size saucepan, combine the sugar and cornstarch. Slowly add the milk, and stir until the sugar dissolves.

4. Cook over low heat, stirring constantly, until the mixture is thick enough to coat a spoon, about 8 minutes.

5. Stir in the pineapple until well blended. Beat the egg yolks until light. (Reserve the whites for the meringue.)

6. Add a small amount of the hot mixture to the egg yolks and blend. Add the yolks to the saucepan and blend. Add the vanilla. Cook, stirring constantly, until the mixture is thickened and will mound slightly when dropped from a spoon, about 5 minutes.

7. Pour the filling into the crust. Spread the meringue over the filling so that none shows through, being careful to seal the edges.

8. Bake for 12 to 15 minutes, or until the meringue is lightly browned. Allow the pie to stand at room temperature until the filling is set, then refrigerate.

MERINGUE

3 egg whites, at room temperature
6 tablespoons sugar

In a medium-size bowl, beat the egg whites until stiff but not dry. Add the sugar, 1 tablespoon at a time, and continue beating until the mixture is thick, glossy, and stands in stiff peaks.

THANKSGIVING PUMPKIN PIE

I have a friend who has a secret vice: he likes to binge on slightly warm pumpkin pie topped with 2 or 3 tablespoons of cold butter. Decadent, but delicious.

½ recipe Butter Crust (see page 27) or Old-Fashioned Lard Crust (see page 30)

1 1-pound can pumpkin (about 2 cups)

1 cup dark brown sugar, firmly packed

2 tablespoons honey

2 eggs, lightly beaten

1 cup heavy or whipping cream

⅔ cup milk

2 teaspoons ground cinnamon*

1 teaspoon ground ginger*

½ teaspoon ground nutmeg*

¼ teaspoon ground cloves*

1. Prepare the Butter or Old-Fashioned Lard Crust dough and roll it out on a lightly floured surface to a thickness of ⅛ inch. Ease it gently into a 9- or 10-inch pie pan. Flute edges as desired and set it aside. *Note:* This filling recipe is generous. When using a 9-inch pie pan, be sure to flute the edges high, to incorporate the filling and avoid spills and drips.

2. Preheat the oven to 400° F.

3. Combine the pumpkin, brown sugar, and honey in a large bowl. Add the eggs and beat well.

4. Stir in the cream and milk until well blended.

5. Add the spices and stir to blend. Pour the filling into the crust and bake for 50 to 60 minutes, or until the filling is set.

*Or substitute 1 scant tablespoon pumpkin pie spice for the four spices listed.

PUMPKIN ICE CREAM PIE

With the amount of cooking to be done at holiday time, a pie that you can make and freeze as much as a week ahead may seem too good to be true. The only problem with this one is that it may not last a week once your family finds out where it is!

1 recipe Gingersnap Crust (see page 33)

1 pint cinnamon ice cream, slightly softened

1 pint vanilla ice cream, slightly softened

1 cup canned pumpkin

⅓ cup sugar

½ teaspoon salt

2 teaspoons pumpkin pie spice

½ teaspoon ground nutmeg

1. Prepare the Gingersnap Crust, reserving 2 tablespoons crumbs for garnish. Set it aside.

2. In a large bowl, beat all the remaining ingredients with an electric mixer until well blended and smooth, about 4 minutes. Pour the filling into the crust, sprinkle with the reserved crumbs, and freeze until firm. To store, wrap the pie well in foil or in a sealed plastic bag and freeze.

SWEET POTATO PIE

Fans of sweet potato pie take sides—some choose the custard variety, similar to a pumpkin pie, some the kind that uses sliced sweet potatoes. We prefer the custard because of its light texture and spicy down-home flavor.

½ recipe Old-Fashioned Lard Crust (see page 30)

1⅔ cups peeled and sliced cooked sweet potatoes, or 1 16-ounce can sweet potatoes, drained

3 tablespoons lightly salted butter, softened

1 cup dark brown sugar, firmly packed

⅓ cup granulated sugar

3 eggs

1½ teaspoons vanilla extract

2 teaspoons ground cinnamon

¾ teaspoon ground nutmeg

½ teaspoon ground dried orange peel

1¼ cups half-and-half

1. Prepare the Old-Fashioned Lard Crust dough and roll it out on a lightly floured surface to a thickness of ⅛ inch. Ease it gently into a 10-inch pie pan. Trim the overhang to 1 inch. Flute the edges as desired. Set it aside.

2. Preheat the oven to 400° F.

3. Mash the sweet potatoes by hand or in the workbowl of a food processor or blender.

4. In a large bowl, cream together the butter and sugars. Add the eggs, one at a time, beating well after each addition.

5. Stir in the mashed sweet potatoes, vanilla, spices, and peel; mix well.

6. Add the half-and-half and blend thoroughly; pour into the crust.

7. Bake for 50 to 60 minutes, or until the filling is set.

AUNT BABY'S GRASSHOPPER PIE

This is what Jessie Lou, my grandmother, would call a "party pie." It's rich, pretty, and a perfect special-occasion dessert. Be sure to use green crème de menthe for a lovely color; or tint the filling yourself with green food coloring. For an extra-special touch, garnish with fresh mint leaves.

1 recipe Oreo Cookie Crust (see page 34)
1 envelope unflavored instant gelatin
½ cup sugar
½ cup cold water
3 eggs, at room temperature, separated
¼ cup crème de menthe
¼ cup crème de cacao
1 cup heavy or whipping cream
Mint leaves for garnish (optional)

1. Prepare the Oreo Cookie Crust, setting aside ¼ cup crumbs for garnish.

2. In the top of a double boiler set over hot water, dissolve the gelatin and ¼ cup of sugar in the ½ cup cold water. Add the egg yolks and beat well. Cook over medium heat until the mixture is thick enough to coat a spoon, about 10 minutes. Remove from the heat and cool slightly.

3. Add the liqueurs and blend. Refrigerate the mixture until it is partially set.

4. Beat the egg whites until stiff but not dry. Continue beating and gradually add the remaining ¼ cup sugar. Beat until the whites stand in stiff peaks. Gently fold the whites into the gelatin mixture until well blended.

5. Whip the cream until it stands in soft peaks and gently fold it, too, into the filling until it is completely incorporated.

6. Pour the filling into the crust. Sprinkle the reserved crumbs over the top, and chill for 4 hours before serving. Garnish with the mint leaves if desired.

WISCONSIN SOUR CREAM RAISIN PIE

Tangy, rich, and sweet, this pie is a midwestern favorite. My mother changed and refined her mother's original recipe over the years, so when this pie was served (as it generally was) during the winter months, it never turned out the same way twice! Nonetheless, I feel I have finally arrived at the ultimate version and pass it along. For those who prefer, rum can be substituted for the brandy or bourbon, but it does tend to overpower the sour cream.

1 9-ounce box raisins (about 2 cups)
½ cup brandy or bourbon
½ cup apple juice
1 tablespoon freshly squeezed lemon juice
½ recipe Butter Crust (see page 27)
2 tablespoons lightly salted butter
2 tablespoons all-purpose flour
¾ cup dark brown sugar, firmly packed
3 eggs, at room temperature, separated
1 cup sour cream
Meringue (recipe follows)

1. Soak the raisins in the brandy or bourbon and the juices overnight, or for at least 4 hours.

2. Preheat the oven to 425° F.

3. Prepare the Butter Crust dough and roll it out on a lightly floured surface to a thickness of ⅛ inch. Ease it gently into a 9-inch pie pan; trim the overhang to 1 inch. Flute the edges as desired. Prick the crust all over with the tines of a fork, and bake it for 20 to 25 minutes, or until the crust is golden. Set it aside to cool. Don't turn off the oven.

4. Melt the butter in a medium-size saucepan over medium heat until sizzling. (Do not allow it to brown.) Add the flour to make a roux (paste) and cook, stirring constantly, 2 to 3 minutes.

5. Lower the heat slightly; add the raisins and brown sugar with their liquid to the roux. Stir until well blended, and cook for 4 minutes or until slightly thickened.

6. Beat the egg yolks until light. (Reserve the whites for the meringue.) Add a small amount of the hot mixture to the egg yolks and blend. Add the yolks to the raisin mixture and cook, stirring constantly, until the mixture is thick enough to coat a spoon. Remove from the heat and allow to cool.

7. Add the sour cream to the cooled raisin mixture, blend well, and pour it into the crust. Spread the meringue over the filling so that none shows through, being careful to seal the edges.

8. Bake for 12 to 15 minutes, or until the

meringue is lightly browned. Set the pie aside for 3 hours before serving.

MERINGUE

3 egg whites, at room temperature
7 tablespoons sugar

In a medium-size bowl, beat the egg whites until stiff but not dry. Gradually add the sugar, 1 tablespoon at a time, beating constantly until the mixture is thick, glossy, and stands in stiff peaks.

RENATA'S ANGEL PIE

As my grandmother (and almost anybody else's) will tell you, the simple things are often the best. The same rule often applies to pies.

1 recipe Meringue Crust (see page 34)
4 egg yolks, lightly beaten
Grated peel of 1 large lemon (about 2 tablespoons)
Juice of 1 large lemon (about ¼ cup)
⅓ cup sugar
1 cup heavy or whipping cream

1. Bake the Meringue Crust, and set it aside.

2. Combine the egg yolks, lemon peel and juice, and the sugar in the top of a double

boiler set over hot water. Cook over medium heat, stirring constantly, until the mixture is thick and mounds slightly when dropped from a spoon, 8 to 10 minutes. Remove from the heat and cool to room temperature.

3. Whip the cream until it stands in soft peaks. Gently fold the cream into the egg-lemon mixture until well blended. Pour it into the meringue crust.

4. Chill several hours or overnight before serving.

BUTTERSCOTCH PIE

½ recipe Basic Pie Crust (see page 25)
2 cups plus 2 tablespoons milk
½ cup dark brown sugar, firmly packed
¼ cup all-purpose flour
½ teaspoon salt
2 eggs, at room temperature, separated
Meringue (recipe follows)

1. Preheat the oven to 425° F.

2. Prepare the Basic Pie Crust dough and roll it out on a lightly floured surface to a thickness of ⅛ inch. Ease it gently into a 9-inch pie pan; trim the overhang to 1 inch. Flute the edges as desired. Prick the crust all over with the tines of a fork, and bake for 20 to 25 minutes, or until the crust is golden. Set it aside to cool. Don't turn off the oven.

3. In a medium-size saucepan, scald 2 cups of the milk by bringing it just to the boiling point. Meanwhile, combine the brown sugar, flour, and salt; stir the dry mixture into the scalded milk until well blended and free of lumps.

4. Cook the mixture over medium heat, stirring constantly, until it is thick enough to coat a spoon, about 5 minutes. Reduce the heat to low.

5. In a small bowl, add the egg yolks to the remaining 2 tablespoons milk and whisk them together until well blended. (Reserve the whites for the meringue.) Add a small portion of the hot mixture to the yolks, then add the yolks to the saucepan. Continue to cook, stirring constantly, until smooth and thick, 5 minutes.

6. Pour the filling into the crust. Spread the meringue over the filling so that none shows through, being careful to seal the edges.

7. Bake for 15 minutes, or until the meringue is lightly browned. Allow the pie to stand at room temperature until the filling is set, then refrigerate.

MERINGUE

2 egg whites, at room temperature
6 tablespoons sugar

In a medium-size bowl, beat the egg whites until stiff but not dry. Gradually add the sugar, 1 tablespoon at a time, until the mixture is thick, glossy, and stands in stiff peaks.

EAST TEXAS MILLIONAIRE PIE

A perfect summer pie—light, sweet, and no baking! Whipped heavy cream can be substituted for the whipped topping here, but the filling and topping will not set as well. When made with whipped cream the pie must be served the same day.

1 recipe Graham Cracker Crust (see page 33)

1 8-ounce package cream cheese, softened

½ cup sugar

1 8-ounce can crushed pineapple, undrained (approximately 1 cup)

1 cup grated coconut

1 cup chopped pecans

1 8-ounce carton prepared whipped topping (see Note)

1. Prepare the Graham Cracker Crust, reserving 4 tablespoons crumbs for garnish. Chill the crust.

2. Whip the softened cream cheese and sugar together until well blended and smooth, about 4 minutes on the high speed of an electric mixer.

3. Stir in the pineapple, coconut, and pecans and mix thoroughly.

PIE FACT

Pioneer women often made as many as fifty pies at a time. In the winter the pies were baked, then stacked and stored in a lean-to or unheated shed to freeze.

4. Gently fold in half of the prepared whipped topping or whipped cream and stir until all the ingredients are well blended. Pour the filling into the crust.

5. Spread the remaining whipped topping evenly over the filling; sprinkle with the reserved crumbs. Chill several hours before serving.

Note: To substitute real whipped cream, whip 2 cups heavy or whipping cream with chilled beaters in a chilled bowl until soft peaks form. Add 4 tablespoons sugar and continue to whip until well blended.

STRAWBERRY-BANANA YOGURT PIE

This is ridiculously easy, sinfully rich, and wonderfully good. In short, even though it might not pass the stricter baking standards of the Kennedy cooks, I recommend it anyway.

1 recipe Graham Cracker Crust (see page 33)

2 8-ounce containers strawberry yogurt with strawberry preserves

1 8-ounce container banana yogurt

1 8-ounce carton prepared whipped topping (see Note)

Fresh strawberries for garnish (optional)

1. Prepare the Graham Cracker Crust, reserving 2 tablespoons crumbs for garnish. Chill the crust.

2. In a large bowl, combine the yogurts until well blended; fold in the whipped topping and stir until thoroughly combined.

3. Spread the filling evenly in the crust. Garnish with fresh strawberries, if desired.

Note: To substitute real whipped cream, whip 2 cups heavy or whipping cream with chilled beaters in a chilled bowl until soft peaks form. Add 4 tablespoons sugar and continue to whip until well blended.

SLIPPED CUSTARD PIE

In this recipe, the custard is baked separately and "slipped" into the crust, guaranteeing a crisp bottom crust that serves as a perfect complement to the rich, smooth filling. Be sure to use a pie pan with smooth sides—glass is best.

½ recipe Butter Crust (see page 27)
4 eggs
1¼ cups light cream or half-and-half
1¼ cups milk
½ cup sugar
1 teaspoon vanilla extract
½ teaspoon ground nutmeg
Sweetened Whipped Cream (see page 77)

1. Preheat the oven to 425° F.

2. Prepare the Butter Crust dough and roll it out on a lightly floured surface to a thickness of ⅛ inch. Ease it gently into a 9-inch pie pan; trim the overhang to 1 inch. Flute the edges as desired. Prick the crust all over with the tines of a fork and bake for 20 to 25 minutes, or until the crust is golden. Set it aside to cool.

3. Reduce the oven temperature to 350° F.

4. Beat the eggs lightly. Add the cream, milk, sugar, and vanilla, and continue beating until all the ingredients are combined and the sugar has dissolved.

5. Generously butter the bottom and sides of a 9-inch pie pan.

6. Pour the filling into the pan; sprinkle it with the nutmeg.

7. Place the pie pan in a larger pan and add enough hot water to come 1½ inches up the sides of the pie pan.

8. Bake for 35 to 40 minutes, or until a knife inserted in the center of the custard comes out clean. Remove it from the oven and remove the pie pan from the larger pan. Allow custard to cool for 10 minutes.

9. Run a thin, sharp knife around the edge of the custard to loosen it. Tap the bottom of the pan sharply three or four times, or until you're sure the custard is not sticking. Align the far edge of the custard pan over the far edge of the crust, tip the custard pan, and slide the custard into the crust. Serve with Sweetened Whipped Cream.

AUNT DEAR'S PECAN CREME PIE

Though the rivalry among the cooks in our family tends to get pretty intense, nobody will argue about this recipe. It's one of the best pecan pie recipes I've ever come across.

½ recipe Basic Pie Crust (see page 25), or
    1 unbaked Make-Ahead Crust (see
    page 26)
¾ cup sugar
2½ tablespoons all-purpose flour
½ teaspoon salt
1 cup light corn syrup
2 eggs
1 5-ounce can evaporated milk
2 teaspoons vanilla extract
1 cup roughly broken pecans

1. If you are using the Basic Pie Crust, prepare the dough and roll it out on a lightly floured surface to a thickness of ⅛ inch. Ease it gently into a 9-inch pie pan and trim the overhang to 1 inch. Flute the edges as desired, and set it aside.

If you are using a Make-Ahead Crust, place it in a pie pan and allow it to defrost.

2. Preheat the oven to 350° F.

3. Combine the sugar, flour, and salt in a large bowl.

4. Add the corn syrup and blend thoroughly. Beat the eggs lightly and add them to the sugar mixture; stir to blend. Add the evaporated milk and stir until blended.

5. Add the vanilla and pecans and mix well. Pour the filling into the crust and bake for 1 hour, or until the filling is set and browned.

PIE FACT

If you want to make pecan pie like a native, be sure not to overcook it. The pecans should form a single layer over the filling, and the pie should be cooked *just until set* in a slow oven. Higher temperatures and overbaking tend to rob the filling of its gooeyness—essential to good pecan pie.

MARK KENNEDY'S PECAN PIE

My younger brother swears by his recipe for pecan pie—one that uses both dark brown sugar and dark corn syrup for a rich, molassesy filling.

½ recipe Basic Pie Crust (see page 25),
    or 1 unbaked Make-Ahead Crust
    (see page 26)

3 eggs

1 cup dark corn syrup

1 cup dark brown sugar, firmly packed

½ teaspoon salt

1 teaspoon vanilla extract

3 tablespoons lightly salted butter, softened

1 cup coarsely chopped pecans

1. If you are using the Basic Pie Crust, prepare the dough and roll it out on a lightly floured surface to a thickness of ⅛ inch. Ease it gently into a 9-inch pie pan; trim the overhang to 1 inch. Flute the edges as desired. Set it aside.

If you are using a Make-Ahead Crust, place it in a pie pan and allow it to defrost.

2. Preheat the oven to 350° F.

3. Place the eggs, corn syrup, brown sugar, salt, vanilla, and butter in a medium-size mixing bowl. Beat for 3 minutes on medium speed with an electric mixer, or by hand until the butter is completely incorporated.

4. Add the pecans and stir to blend. Pour the filling into the crust and bake for 1 hour.

SOUTHERN PEANUT PIE

With a hearty, old-fashioned lard crust (not recommended for the cholesterol conscious!), this is a great-tasting and economical nut pie. In fact, many people prefer it to the more expensive pecan.

½ recipe Old-Fashioned Lard Crust (see page 30)

3 eggs

½ cup sugar

1½ cups dark corn syrup

4 tablespoons (¼ cup) lightly salted butter, melted

1 teaspoon vanilla extract

1 cup chopped roasted unsalted peanuts

1. Prepare the Old-Fashioned Lard Crust dough and roll it out on a lightly floured surface to a thickness of ⅛ inch. Ease it gently into a 10-inch pie pan and flute the edges as desired. (If you use a 9-inch pie pan, flute the edges high enough to hold the filling and add 5 minutes to the baking time.) Set it aside.

2. Preheat the oven to 375° F.

3. Beat the eggs, sugar, and corn syrup together in a large bowl for 3 minutes with an electric mixer on medium speed. Continue beating, adding the melted butter in a thin stream until well blended. Add the vanilla and stir to blend.

4. Add the chopped peanuts and blend thoroughly. Pour into the crust.

5. Bake for 45 minutes, or until the filling is set.

CHOCOLATE PECAN PIE

Rich, rich, rich! Serve in thin wedges even to skinny people.

½ recipe Basic Pie Crust (see page 25), or 1 unbaked Make-Ahead Crust (see page 26)

1 cup sugar

½ teaspoon salt

2 tablespoons all-purpose flour

¾ cup dark corn syrup

3 eggs

¾ cup chopped pecans

6 ounces semi-sweet chocolate, broken into small pieces, or 6 ounces chocolate chips

Unsweetened Whipped Cream (recipe follows)

1. If you are using the Basic Pie Crust, prepare the dough and roll it out on a lightly floured surface to a thickness of ⅛ inch. Ease it gently into a 9-inch pie pan; trim the overhang to 1 inch. Flute the edges as desired. Set it aside.

If you are using a Make-Ahead Crust, place it in a pie pan and allow it to defrost.

2. Preheat the oven to 375° F.

3. In a medium-size bowl, sift together the sugar, salt, and flour. Add the corn syrup and stir to blend.

4. Add the eggs, one at a time, beating well after each addition.

5. Stir in the nuts and chocolate; pour the filling into the crust.

6. Bake for 50 to 60 minutes, or until the filling is set. Top with Unsweetened Whipped Cream.

UNSWEETENED WHIPPED CREAM

1 cup heavy or whipping cream

Thoroughly chill the mixing bowl and beaters. Whip the cream in the bowl with a hand-held mixer at high speed until soft peaks form, about 2 to 3 minutes. (Don't use ultrapasteurized "keeps for weeks"–type heavy cream for whipped cream. It often lacks flavor and can fail to whip properly.)

FRENCH CHOCOLATE SILK PIE

No one really knows where this recipe originated, or why it's called "French," but each side of my family boasts at least three different versions of this remarkably easy and elegant pie.

1 recipe Oreo Cookie Crust (see page 34), or ½ recipe Butter Crust (see page 27) or Pecan Crust (see page 32)

3 ounces unsweetened chocolate

8 tablespoons (½ cup) unsalted butter, softened

¾ cup sugar

2 eggs

1½ teaspoons vanilla extract

Kahlua Whipped Cream (optional; recipe follows)

1. Prepare the Oreo Cookie Crust, reserving ¼ cup crumbs as garnish. Chill the crust.

If you are using the Butter or Pecan Crust, preheat the oven to 425° F. Prepare the dough and roll it out on a lightly floured surface to a thickness of ⅛ inch. Ease it into a 9-inch pie pan, and trim the overhang to 1 inch. Flute the edges as desired.

Prick the pastry all over with the tines of a fork and bake it for 25 minutes, or until lightly browned. Set it aside to cool.

2. In a small saucepan, melt the chocolate over very low heat; set it aside.

3. Meanwhile, whip the butter until very light. Gradually add the sugar, beating constantly until the mixture is light and fluffy, about 5 minutes with a hand-held mixer on high speed.

4. Add the eggs and continue beating for 4 minutes on high speed.

5. Add the vanilla and the melted chocolate. Continue beating on high speed until no sugar granules remain, approximately 8 minutes.

6. Pour the mixture into the crust and sprinkle on the reserved crumbs. Chill the pie for at least 1 hour before serving. If desired, top with Kahlua Whipped Cream.

KAHLUA WHIPPED CREAM

1 cup heavy or whipping cream
2 tablespoons confectioners' sugar
2 tablespoons Kahlua

1. Thoroughly chill the mixing bowl and beaters of an electric mixer. Whip the cream in the bowl until soft peaks form.

2. Add the sugar and Kahlua and continue beating until the mixture is thoroughly blended and stands in peaks. Serve immediately over the chilled pie.

BLACK MAGIC PIE

½ recipe Pecan Crust (see page 32)
6 ounces unsweetened chocolate, broken into pieces
1¼ cups confectioners' sugar
2 tablespoons lightly salted butter
2 tablespoons hot water
2 eggs, separated, at room temperature
1⅓ cups heavy or whipping cream
Whole pecans, for garnish
Unsweetened Whipped Cream (see page 73), for garnish

1. Preheat the oven to 400°F.

2. Prepare the Pecan Crust dough and roll it out on a lightly floured surface to a thickness of ¼ inch. Ease it gently into a 9-inch pie pan, and trim the overhang to 1 inch. Flute the edges as desired. Prick the crust all over with the tines of a fork, and bake for 20 to 25 minutes, or until the crust is golden. Set it aside to cool.

3. Melt the chocolate in the top of a double boiler over boiling water until smooth. Add the sugar, butter, and hot water; stir until well blended (mixture will be thick).

4. Beat the egg yolks until light; add a small portion of the chocolate mixture to the yolks and blend. Add the yolks to the double boiler and continue cooking, stirring constantly, for 4 minutes. Remove the double boiler from the heat and allow the mixture to cool to lukewarm.

5. Beat the egg whites until stiff. Gently fold them into the chocolate mixture until well blended.

6. Whip the cream until soft peaks form. Gently fold the whipped cream into the chocolate mixture.

7. Pour the mixture into the cooled pecan crust and chill the pie for at least 3 hours, or until set. Garnish with pecans and Unsweetened Whipped Cream as desired.

CHOCOLATE CREAM PIE

For the real chocolate lovers among you—chocolate filling plus a chocolate crust, plus a chocolate garnish.

1 recipe Oreo Cookie Crust (see page 34)

2 cups milk

2 ounces unsweetened chocolate, broken into pieces

3½ tablespoons cornstarch

⅔ cup sugar

2 egg yolks

½ teaspoon rum extract

Sweetened Whipped Cream (recipe follows)

Chocolate Curls (optional; see page 79)

1. Prepare the Oreo Cookie Crust, reserving ¼ cup crumbs for garnish.

2. Place the milk and the chocolate in a medium-size saucepan, and cook over low heat until the chocolate is slightly melted and the mixture is steaming.

3. Meanwhile, combine the cornstarch and sugar thoroughly in a small bowl. When the chocolate mixture is steaming, add the dry mixture to the pan and blend.

4. Cook over low heat, stirring constantly, until the chocolate melts completely and the mixture is thick enough to mound slightly when dropped from a spoon, 8 to 10 minutes.

5. Beat the egg yolks until light; add a small amount of the hot chocolate mixture to the egg yolks and blend. Pour the yolks into the pan and blend. Cook, stirring constantly, 3 to 4 minutes. Remove from the heat.

6. Add the rum extract and stir to blend. Pour the filling into the crust and sprinkle on the reserved crumbs. Chill the pie for at least 1 hour before spreading it with the Sweetened Whipped Cream.

7. Top the whipped cream with Chocolate Curls, if desired. Refrigerate until serving.

SWEETENED WHIPPED CREAM

1 cup heavy or whipping cream
2 tablespoons sugar
1 teaspoon vanilla extract

1. Thoroughly chill the mixing bowl and beaters of an electric mixer. Whip the cream in the bowl until soft peaks form.

2. Add the sugar and vanilla. Continue whipping until well blended.

BLACK BOTTOM PIE

Admittedly complicated, but one of the greats. This version evolved from one developed by Chef Carson Gulley of the University of Wisconsin. At one time my mother worked on his staff, and she brought his touch of rum and addition of bittersweet chocolate to her own recipe for this pie. Traditional black bottom pies have a layer of chocolate custard over the crust, topped by a vanilla custard. We prefer bittersweet chocolate, melted and spread in a thick layer over the crust, topped by a chiffon-type custard.

½ recipe Basic Pie Crust (see page 25), or
    1 baked Make-Ahead Crust (see page 26)

4 ounces bittersweet chocolate

2 tablespoons lightly salted butter

1 teaspoon rum extract

⅔ cup sugar

3½ tablespoons cornstarch

½ teaspoon salt

1 envelope unflavored gelatin

⅓ cup cold water

2 cups milk

2 tablespoons dark rum

4 eggs, at room temperature, separated

1 cup heavy or whipping cream

4 tablespoons light corn syrup

Chocolate Curls (recipe follows)

1. If you are using the Basic Pie Crust, preheat the oven to 425° F. Prepare the dough and roll it out on a lightly floured surface to a thickness of ⅛ inch. Ease it gently into a 9-inch pie pan; trim the overhang to 1 inch. Flute the edges as desired. Prick all over with the tines of a fork and bake for 20 to 25 minutes, or until the crust is golden.

If you are using the Make-Ahead Crust, place it in a pie pan and allow it to defrost.

2. Combine the chocolate, butter, and rum extract in a small saucepan and cook over low heat, stirring constantly, until the chocolate has melted and the mixture is smooth.

3. Spread the chocolate mixture in a thick layer over the bottom and sides of the crust. (This is easier if the crust is still warm from the oven.)

4. Reserve 5 tablespoons of the sugar and set it aside. Sift the remaining sugar with the cornstarch and salt into the top of a double boiler.

5. Dissolve the gelatin in the cold water and set aside to soften for 5 minutes.

6. Add the milk and rum to the sugar mixture and stir until the sugar dissolves. Cook over hot water on medium heat until the mixture is thick enough to coat a spoon and has lost any starchy flavor, about 10 minutes.

7. Beat the egg yolks until light; reserve the whites. Add a small amount of the hot milk mixture to the egg yolks and blend well. Then add the yolk mixture to the pan; blend well. Continue cooking until the mixture is thick and will mound slightly when dropped from a spoon, about 5 minutes.

8. Add the gelatin and stir. Continue cooking for 5 minutes, stirring constantly. Make sure that all the gelatin granules have completely dissolved. Remove from the heat and chill until partially set, stirring occasionally.

9. Whip the egg whites until stiff but not dry. Gradually add the reserved 5 tablespoons sugar, 1 tablespoon at a time, and continue beating until the meringue mixture stands in stiff peaks. Divide approximately in half.

10. Stir half the meringue into the partially set custard; blend well. Gently fold the remaining meringue into the mixture until thoroughly incorporated.

11. Pour the filling into the crust. Chill the pie for 1 hour.

12. Whip the cream until soft peaks form. Add the corn syrup in a thin stream, beating until well blended. Spread the whipped cream evenly over the filled pie. Top with chocolate curls.

CHOCOLATE CURLS

This is the shortcut method for curling chocolate. All you need is a piece of chocolate and a swivel-bladed vegetable peeler.

1 piece dark or semi-sweet chocolate, about 4 x 1¾ inches

1. Allow the chocolate to sit in a warm place for 15 minutes or until it can be cut without crumbling. (On a saucer over the pilot light on the stove is great.)

2. Place the chocolate flat side up in the palm of your hand. Press the peeler down firmly at the far end of the chocolate and move it toward you, lengthwise along the chocolate. Place the curls on a plate and chill until firm, about 20 minutes.

BUTTERMILK PIE

An old-fashioned recipe that might seem unusual to pie eaters today. The custard filling is tangy and sweet, reminiscent of pies made with cream cheese. For an interesting variation, substitute lemon extract for the vanilla and nutmeg.

½ recipe Basic Pie Crust (see page 25), or
    1 unbaked Make-Ahead Crust (see
    page 26)

2 cups buttermilk

3 tablespoons all-purpose flour

3 tablespoons lightly salted butter, melted

⅔ cup sugar

2 eggs

1 teaspoon vanilla extract

½ teaspoon ground nutmeg

1. If you are using the Basic Pie Crust, prepare the dough and roll it out on a lightly floured surface to a thickness of ⅛ inch. Ease it gently into a 9-inch pie pan; trim the overhang to 1 inch. Flute the edges as desired. Set it aside.

    If you are using a Make-Ahead Crust, place it in a pie pan and allow it to defrost.

2. Preheat the oven to 425° F.

3. In a large mixing bowl, combine the buttermilk, flour, and melted butter and beat until the flour is completely blended. Add the sugar and continue beating.

PIE FACT

The Pennsylvania Dutch first came up with the marvelous concoctions we know as custard pies. The settlers, however, called them "nervous pies," because of the way the delicate custards quivered in the crust.

4. Add the eggs, one at a time, beating well after each addition. Add the vanilla and blend.

5. Pour the filling into the crust and sprinkle it with the nutmeg. Bake for 10 minutes.

6. Reduce the oven temperature to 350° F and bake for an additional 20 to 25 minutes, or until the filling is set. Serve warm or chilled.

DEPRESSION OATMEAL PIE WITH CINNAMON CRUST

Family legend has it that this pie first became popular during the Depression, when folks were so poor they couldn't afford pecans even in those areas of the country where they were plentiful. I've retained the title but have a different explanation: One taste of this rich, spicy confection will cheer anybody up.

CRUST

½ recipe Butter Crust (see page 27)

2 teaspoons ground cinnamon

2 tablespoons sugar

FILLING

4 tablespoons lightly salted butter, softened

⅔ cup light brown sugar, firmly packed

1 teaspoon ground cinnamon

½ teaspoon ground cloves

1 cup light corn syrup

3 eggs

1 cup quick oatmeal

1. Prepare the Butter Crust dough, adding the cinnamon and sugar to the dry ingredients. Roll it out on a lightly floured surface to a thickness of ⅛ inch and ease it into a 9-inch pie pan. Trim the overhang to 1 inch. Flute the edges as desired. Set it aside.

2. Preheat the oven to 350° F.

3. In a medium-size bowl, cream together the butter, sugar, and spices until well blended.

4. Add the corn syrup and blend well. Add the eggs, one at a time, beating well after each addition.

5. Stir in the oatmeal and pour the mixture into the crust. Bake for 1 hour, or until the filling is set.

LEMON WONDER BREAD PIE

W hat could be more American than Wonder Bread? Actually this is an updated version of a recipe that dates from the time of the pioneers. Frontier women used stale bread as a means of thickening pie filling and stretching ingredients.

½ recipe Butter Crust (see page 27) or
  Basic Pie Crust (see page 25)

5 slices Wonder Bread or other light bread,
  crusts removed

½ cup hot water, approximately

1 cup sugar

½ cup freshly squeezed lemon juice (about
  2 large lemons)

2 tablespoons freshly grated lemon peel
  (about 2 large lemons)

3 eggs, at room temperature, separated

2 tablespoons lightly salted butter, softened

Meringue (recipe follows)

1. Preheat the oven to 425° F.

2. Prepare the Butter or Basic Pie Crust dough and roll it out on a lightly floured surface to a thickness of ⅛ inch. Gently ease it into a 9-inch pie pan; trim the overhang to 1 inch. Flute the edges as desired. Prick the crust all over with the tines of a fork and bake for 20 to 25 minutes, or until the crust is golden. Set aside to cool. Don't turn off the oven.

3. Tear the bread slices into pieces and soak them in the hot water until mushy. Squeeze lightly to remove any excess water and place the bread in a medium-size saucepan.

4. Add the sugar, lemon juice and peel, and the egg yolks. (Reserve the whites for the meringue.) Beat with a hand-held electric mixer for 3 minutes on high speed.

5. Cook the mixture over low heat, stirring constantly, until it is thick enough to coat a spoon, about 8 minutes. Remove from the heat.

6. Add the butter and beat on high speed for 2 minutes, or until the mixture is light, smooth, and thick. Pour it into the crust. Spread the meringue evenly over the filling so that none shows through, being careful to seal the edges.

7. Bake for 12 to 15 minutes, or until the meringue is lightly browned. Allow the pie to stand at room temperature until the filling is set, then chill.

MERINGUE

3 egg whites, at room temperature

¼ cup sugar

In a medium-size bowl, beat the egg whites until stiff but not dry. Continue beating and gradually add the sugar, 1 tablespoon at a time. Beat until the mixture is thick, glossy, and stands in stiff peaks.

APPLE COCONUT PAN PIE

This recipe comes from my maternal grandmother, Renata, who was a great party-giver and gained something of a reputation as a fine hostess. Grandma learned from the time she was first married to cook for large groups of hungry people, and she often served pies for dessert. Her pan pies are pies for a crowd, usually baked in large, oblong baking dishes. This one uses no bottom crust, but is topped with a buttery, rich cookie crust.

Pan Pie Top Crust (recipe follows)

7 cups sliced apples (about 3 pounds
    before peeling and coring)

⅓ cup all-purpose flour

1 cup sugar

2 teaspoons ground cinnamon

1 teaspoon ground nutmeg

1½ cups shredded coconut

4 tablespoons (¼ cup) lightly salted butter

½ cup light cream or half-and-half

1. Prepare the Pan Pie Top Crust dough, and set it aside.

2. Preheat the oven to 375° F.

3. In a large bowl, toss the apple slices with the flour, sugar, spices, and coconut until well coated. Arrange the mixture evenly in a rectangular baking pan measuring 9 x 13 x 2 inches.

4. Dot the apple slices with the butter, then pour the cream over all.

5. Lay the crust evenly over the filling and fold the edges under to seal. Flute as desired. Cut slits at intervals in the crust to allow steam to escape.

6. Bake for 45 minutes, or until the apples test tender and the crust is lightly browned. Serve warm with Sweetened Whipped Cream (see page 77) or ice cream.

PAN PIE TOP CRUST

2 cups all-purpose flour

4½ tablespoons sugar

½ teaspoon baking powder

2 sticks (1 cup) lightly salted butter, chilled,
    cut into small pieces

2 egg yolks

5 to 6 tablespoons ice water

1. Sift the dry ingredients together in a large bowl. Cut in the butter and work the mixture with your fingertips or a pastry blender until it has the texture of coarse crumbs.

2. Beat the egg yolks with 5 tablespoons water. Add this to the flour mixture and work the mixture until all the ingredients are moistened and the dough can be shaped. Add more water only if necessary.

3. Place the dough on a lightly floured surface and roll it out into a rectangle approximately 14 x 10 x ¼ inch. Loosen the dough from the work surface, wrap it loosely around the rolling pin, and set it aside.

AUNT BABY'S BLUEBERRY CREAM CHEESE PAN PIE

1 Pan Pie Bottom Crust (recipe follows)

2 8-ounce packages cream cheese, softened

⅔ cup sugar

2 teaspoons vanilla extract

¼ cup light cream or half-and-half

2½ cups fresh Blueberry Filling (recipe follows), or 1 can prepared blueberry filling

2 cups sour cream

½ cup confectioners' sugar

1. Prepare and bake the Pan Pie Bottom Crust. Set it aside to cool.

2. Beat together the softened cream cheese, sugar, vanilla, and light cream until the mixture is very light and no sugar granules remain.

3. Spread the mixture over the crust. Top with Blueberry Filling.

4. Combine the sour cream and confectioners' sugar. Spread over the Blueberry Filling. Chill thoroughly before serving.

PAN PIE BOTTOM CRUST

2 cups all-purpose flour

1 teaspoon salt

4 tablespoons sugar

⅔ cup lightly salted butter, chilled, cut into small pieces

3 to 4 tablespoons milk

1. Preheat the oven to 425° F.

2. In a large bowl, sift together the dry ingredients. Cut in the butter and blend it with your fingertips or a pastry blender until the mixture has the texture of coarse crumbs.

3. Sprinkle the milk over the surface of the crumb mixture and blend until all the ingredients are moistened and the dough can be shaped. Press it into the bottom of a 9 x 13 x 2-inch baking pan. Bake for 20 minutes, or until crisp and golden. Cool.

BLUEBERRY FILLING

1 pint fresh blueberries

⅔ cup sugar

2 tablespoons freshly squeezed lemon juice

3½ tablespoons cornstarch

⅓ cup cold water

1. Wash, drain, and sort the berries, discarding any bruised or unripe fruit.

2. Combine the berries, sugar, and lemon juice in a medium-size saucepan and cook over medium heat until the sugar has dissolved and the berries have begun to give off their juice.

3. In a small bowl, combine the cornstarch and cold water and stir well; add to the berry mixture and cook, stirring constantly, until the mixture is no longer cloudy and mounds slightly when dropped from a spoon. Cool.

Makes 2½ cups.

OLD-FASHIONED HOOSIER CREAM PIE

A treasure of a recipe given to me by my Indiana friend Trish Earley, whose family has been using it for generations. I guarantee that once you taste it, you'll understand why everybody calls them the good old days!

½ recipe Basic Pie Crust (see page 25) or
Indestructible Pie Crust (see page 29)
4 tablespoons all-purpose flour
¼ teaspoon salt
¾ cup sugar
½ teaspoon ground nutmeg (optional)
2 cups light cream
Ground cinnamon

1. Prepare the Basic or Indestructible Crust dough and roll it out on a lightly floured surface to a thickness of ⅛ inch. Ease it gently into a 9-inch pie pan, and trim the overhang to 1 inch. Flute the edges as desired and set it aside.

2. Preheat the oven to 425° F.

3. Mix the flour, salt, sugar, and nutmeg in a small bowl and spread the mixture over the bottom of the crust. Pour in the cream, and sprinkle it with the cinnamon.

4. Invert a second pie pan over the top and place them in the oven. Bake for 25 minutes.

5. Uncover the pie and continue baking an additional 20 to 25 minutes, or until the filling is set and lightly browned. Allow the pie to stand at room temperature for 20 minutes before serving. (The filling will appear thick and bubbly around the edges when this pie is done. It will continue to thicken and set as the pie cools.)

DRUNKEN CHESS PIE

This "secret" family recipe has been much requested as a donation to PTA and church bake sales in Jessie Lou's neck of the woods. I daresay once the ingredients are made public it will raise the eyebrows (and the spirits) of more than a few of the congregation!

½ recipe Basic Pie Crust (see page 25), or 1 unbaked Make-Ahead Crust (see page 26)

1½ cups sugar

2½ tablespoons all-purpose flour

8 tablespoons (½ cup) lightly salted butter, softened

3 eggs

⅓ cup good-quality sour mash bourbon

¼ cup light cream or half-and-half

1 teaspoon vanilla extract

1 teaspoon rum extract

Unsweetened Whipped Cream (see page 73)

1. If you are using the Basic Pie Crust, prepare the dough and roll it out on a lightly floured surface to a thickness of ⅛ inch. Ease it gently into a 9-inch pie pan; trim the overhang to 1 inch. Flute the edges as desired, and set it aside.

If you are using the Make-Ahead Crust, place it in a pie pan and allow it to defrost.

PIE FACT

The Southern specialties known as chess pies have a number of theories associated with their unusual name. One is that "chess" is Southern for chest, and that the rich sugary pies were the keeping pies of the Old South—those that could be stored without refrigeration. Another legend says that nine out of ten times when you ask a Southerner "What's for dessert?" you'll get the reply, "Jes' pie."

2. Preheat the oven to 375° F.

3. In a medium-size bowl, cream together the sugar, flour, and butter.

4. Add the eggs, one at a time, beating well after each addition.

5. Add the bourbon, cream, and extracts, and stir to blend. Pour the filling into the crust.

6. Bake for 50 to 60 minutes, or until the filling is set and lightly browned. To serve, top with Unsweetened Whipped Cream.

TRANSPARENT PIE

Another variation of chess pie, this time with cream and coconut.

½ recipe Basic Pie Crust (see page 25), or
1 unbaked Make-Ahead Crust (see page 26)

2 cups sugar

2½ tablespoons all-purpose flour

3 eggs

8 tablespoons (½ cup) lightly salted butter, softened

1 cup light cream or half-and-half

1 teaspoon vanilla extract

½ cup shredded coconut

1. If you are using the Basic Pie Crust, prepare the dough and roll it out on a lightly floured surface to a thickness of ⅛ inch. Ease it gently into a 9-inch pie pan; trim the overhang to 1 inch. Flute the edges as desired, and set it aside.

If you are using the Make-Ahead Crust, place it in a pie pan and allow it to defrost.

2. Preheat the oven to 375° F.

3. In a medium-size bowl, combine the sugar and flour.

4. Add the eggs, one at a time, beating well after each addition. Continue beating by hand or with an electric mixer on high speed until the mixture is very light and thick, about 3 minutes.

5. Add the butter and beat until well blended. Add the cream in a thin stream and continue beating until the ingredients are thoroughly combined. Stir in the vanilla and coconut to blend.

6. Pour the filling into the crust and bake for 50 to 60 minutes, or until the filling is set. Serve warm or cold.

BROWN SUGAR VINEGAR PIE

Another recipe that dates from a bygone era—cider vinegar adds a tang to a gooey sweet filling. For added flavor and texture, sprinkle with chopped walnuts or pecans before baking.

½ recipe Old-Fashioned Lard Crust (see page 30) or Basic Pie Crust (see page 25)

8 tablespoons (½ cup) lightly salted butter, softened

2 tablespoons all-purpose flour

1 cup dark brown sugar, firmly packed

½ cup granulated sugar

3 eggs

¼ cup apple juice

¼ cup cider vinegar

¼ cup chopped walnuts or pecans (optional)

Unsweetened Whipped Cream (see page 73)

1. Prepare the Old-Fashioned Lard or Basic Pie Crust dough and roll it out on a lightly floured surface to a thickness of ⅛ inch. Ease it gently into a 9-inch pie pan; trim the overhang to 1 inch. Flute the edges as desired. Set it aside.

2. Preheat the oven to 375° F.

3. In a medium-size bowl, cream together the butter, flour, and sugars until light.

4. Add the eggs, one at a time, beating well after each addition.

5. Stir in the apple juice and vinegar and blend. Pour the filling into the crust and sprinkle with the chopped nuts if desired.

6. Bake for 50 to 60 minutes, or until the filling is set and a knife inserted into the center comes out clean. To serve, top with Unsweetened Whipped Cream.

SHOOFLY PIE

Shoofly Pie originated in the kitchens of the Pennsylvania Dutch. This is a layered version that comes from an Italian friend who lives in Chicago. How's that for a melting pot?

½ recipe Old-Fashioned Lard Crust (see page 30)

½ cup sugar

1½ cups all-purpose flour

1 teaspoon ground cinnamon

½ cup shortening

½ cup hot water

½ cup blackstrap molasses

½ teaspoon baking soda

1. Prepare the Old-Fashioned Lard Crust dough and roll it out on a lightly floured surface to a thickness of ⅛ inch. Ease it gently into a 10-inch pie pan; trim the overhang to 1 inch. Flute the edges as desired.

2. Preheat the oven to 375° F.

3. Sift together the sugar, flour, and cinnamon in a large bowl. Cut in the shortening and blend until the mixture has the consistency of coarse crumbs.

4. In a small bowl, combine the hot water, molasses, and baking soda, and stir until well blended. Working quickly, spread layers of crumbs alternating with layers of the molasses mixture in the crust, beginning and ending with a layer of crumbs.

5. Bake for 40 to 45 minutes, or until the crust is lightly browned and the filling is puffed.

INDEX